Memories of Underdevelopment

Memories of Underdevelopment

THE REVOLUTIONARY FILMS OF CUBA

Edited by Michael Myerson

Grossman Publishers / New York / 1973

First published in 1973 in a hardbound and paperbound edition by
Grossman Publishers, 625 Madison Avenue
New York, N.Y. 10022
Published simultaneously in Canada by
Fitzhenry and Whiteside Ltd.
SBN 670-46827-4 (hardbound)
    670-46828-2 (paperbound)
Library of Congress Catalogue Card Number: 72-93281
Printed in U.S.A.

Acknowledgment
The editor wishes to thank Margaret Randall for permission
to use her translation of the poem by Otto René Castillo which
appears on page 41.

For us, a revolutionary people in a revolutionary process, the value of cultural and artistic creations is determined by their usefulness for the people, by what they contribute to man, by what they contribute to the liberation and happiness of man.

Our standards are political. There cannot be aesthetic value without human content or in opposition to man, justice, welfare, liberation, and the happiness of man.

Fidel Castro

For the brothers and sisters of Cuba's ICAIC
with gratitude and solidarity

Note: I should acknowledge the Treasury Department's own Stanley Sommerfield, who helped make this book necessary. Perhaps Stanley will gather encouragement in his work from these words of Ellsworth Bunker, Ambassador to Saigon, to a fellow Yale alumnus: "The class of 1916 is behind the President's policy."

Contents

Memories of Underdevelopment

Introduction

In his address, Mr. [Eliot] Richardson, retiring as Under-secretary of State, warned against acceptance of what he called "simplistic slogans" such as "No More Vietnams."

The New York Times

To consider Cuban film, one must consider, for example, the following:

On the evening of June 17, 1972, five men were arrested in an attempted raid on the Democratic National Committee office in Washington, D.C. Electronic eavesdropping devices and microfilm photographing equipment were found on the suspects when they were busted. Those arrested included Bernard L. Barker, a wealthy Cuban-born Miami realtor, with investments in Panama, Nicaragua, Chile, and Santo Domingo, who, using the code name "Macho," was the quartermaster for the Central

Intelligence Agency's 1961 invasion of Cuba at Playa Girón (the Bay of Pigs). Joining Barker in the raid was James W. Mc-Cord, Jr., former FBI agent, then for nineteen years a CIA man, rising in that agency to head up its security; also a lieutenant colonel in the Air Force Reserve; at the time of arrest the security chief for the Republican National Committee while moonlighting in the same capacity for the Committee to Re-Elect the President; a member of the sixteen-man U.S. Military Reserve unit which prepares plans for the wartime information security program (including surveillance and list-gathering of domestic radicals) which operates under the Office of Emergency Plans and Preparedness, part of the President's executive office; and finally, but not incidentally, a veteran of the Playa Girón invasion team. Arrested also were Frank A. Sturgis, Virgilio Gonzales, and Eugenio R. Martinez, all of Miami, all with CIA connections, all participants in the Girón aggression.*

Later, submitting himself for arrest was E. Howard Hunt, Jr., a former CIA official, business partner with Barker in various Latin American ventures, up to the time of the raid a member of the White House staff, and overall director for the CIA of the ill-fated invasion of Cuba. *The New York Times* reported five days after the arrests that an organization of Cuban veterans who served in the U.S. Army after participating in the Bay of Pigs operation was involved in the raid. This group, composed of veterans of the 800 Cubans trained at Fort Jackson, S.C., is known by the Spanish name of Ex-Combatientes Cubanos de

---

* This essay was first written in July 1972, only a month after the Watergate case first broke and the original set of burglars was arrested. Since then, of course, a good deal more of that particular iceberg has come to the surface, implicating the President of the United States, his most trusted friends and lieutenants, the FBI, CIA, Securities and Exchange Commission, and many of the major U.S. corporations in a conspiracy against the democratic liberties of the people of our country. Which all the more serves to make the point of this Introduction, explaining how revolutionary Cubans view us and why they make the sort of films they do. This and all subsequent footnotes were added in May 1973, upon reading galley proofs.

Fort Jackson. Both Martinez and Gonzales had links with the Combatientes, whose president, Angel Ferrer, was also at the Watergate apartments the night of the raid. The Watergate houses the Democratic Party offices.*

After the arrests, at three o'clock in the morning, when her husband hadn't called, Barker's wife in Miami called Washington attorney Douglas Caddy, a close friend of Hunt and a founder of the right-wing Young Americans for Freedom, on pre-arranged instructions from Hunt should Barker find himself in difficulties. Caddy was soon found in contempt of court for refusing to answer grand jury questions. Barker's new attorney was Henry Rothblatt, who in 1969 successfully defended Colonel Robert Rheault and five other officers of the U.S. Army's Special Forces on charges that they had murdered a Vietnamese double agent. That trial ended in dismissal of the charges when the CIA refused to allow its agents to testify about its operations in Vietnam in conjunction with the Green Berets. Also joining the defense team was F. Lee Bailey,† who won acquittal for Captain Ernest Medina in his trial, stemming from the My Lai massacre in Vietnam. Telephone records later showed that at least fifteen calls from Barker's home and office were made to an unlisted number in the office of G. Gordon Liddy, attorney for the Committee to Re-Elect the President. Liddy was later arrested for the break-in.

Former Attorney General John N. Mitchell, then head of the

---

* Other Cubans were involved in related activities, including the burglary of the offices housing Daniel Ellsberg's psychiatrist, a break-in ordered by the White House to build a case against Ellsberg, who released the Pentagon Papers. Subsequent news interviews with Cuban exile participants, and exile public opinion in Miami, show that the exiles had come to believe that this was a CIA operation, approved of by the President, because of alleged millions of dollars being fed to the George McGovern presidential campaign by the government of Fidel Castro. Such an allegation could only be believed by minds capable of fantasies of a return of the *ancien regime* to Cuba.

† Bailey was himself indicted on May 18, 1973, on 28 counts of mail fraud and conspiracy in a case unrelated to Watergate.

Committee to Re-Elect the President, had his share of problems. His attempts to dodge accusing fingers were complicated by his wife's outspoken denunciation of his political affairs. In response to a UPI question, during a telephone interview she initiated, regarding the Watergate raid, she said, "I gave him an ultimatum to get out of politics. I'm sick and tired of the whole operation." The phone conversation ended abruptly when it appeared that somebody had taken the phone from her hand and the connection was broken. Subsequent attempts to reach her were to no avail. Mr. Mitchell, mimicking the Duke of Windsor, soon resigned his position, the high point of his public career.* Meanwhile, a million-dollar damage suit was filed by the Democrats against the Nixon re-election committee. Mitchell had initially called the suit a political stunt, but lawyers for the committee asked the district court to postpone hearings on the suit until after the election on grounds that they would cause "incalculable" damage to President Nixon's campaign.

When the Watergate defendants finally came to trial, after the President's re-election, Liddy and McCord were found guilty after an hour and a half of deliberation by the jury. Hunt and the other four had earlier pleaded guilty on all counts in order to, as columnist Jack Anderson and others suggested, escape questioning as to who really ordered and paid for the operation. They needn't have worried. The Nixon-appointed prosecutor never got around to such a line of questioning in the Liddy-McCord trial.† Although one witness did mention Mitch-

---

* Once Grand Dragon of the law-and-order klan, Mitchell was indicted on May 10, 1973, together with former Secretary of Commerce Maurice Stans, on charges of obstructing justice by accepting secret cash contributions in exchange for an effort to influence a Securities and Exchange Commission investigation of Robert L. Vesco, the financier. Further indictments of Mitchell and Stans are the subject of widespread press speculation.

† James McCord later became a chief witness against the White House in testimony before federal grand juries and the Senate committee investigating Watergate.

ell as having approved almost a quarter of a million dollars for political espionage, Liddy claimed not to know from where or whom his bundle came. The financial investigation first came to light through a twenty-five-thousand-dollar check given by Nixon Midwest fundraiser Kenneth Dahlberg to Maurice Stans, Nixon's financial chairman and former Secretary of Commerce, which found its way into Barker's Miami bank account.

Throughout the sordid affair, the President of course sought to disassociate himself from any responsibility. White House Press Secretary Ron Ziegler, former public relations man for Disneyland, called the Watergate raid "a third-rate burglary attempt," implying that if the President were to pull off such a job it would be done to perfection. The press graciously declined to point out that the Bay of Pigs invasion, initiated in the first place by then-Vice-President Nixon and under the guidance of the Watergate heisters, was a third-rate operation. But nobody in public office or the press argued that Nixon wouldn't organize or cover up burglaries because he is an honorable, decent man, highly sensitive to fair play, a defender of law and order.* Nixon has always faked one thing perfectly clear: his election campaigning for twenty-six years is a textbook example of political knees to the groin and thumbs in the eye.

If citizens of this country are skeptical, one can guess what the people of Cuba might think, what connections they might draw between President Nixon, the CIA, and the more reactionary elements of the Cuban exile community in Miami. Playa Girón, for Cuba, was the height of U.S. imperialist villainy, the defeat of which is one of the great moments of Cuban history. It was the first time in two hundred years of the Monroe Doctrine and a century of gunboat diplomacy in the hemisphere that the United States was defeated.

* Indeed, later public opinion polls demonstrate that most U.S. citizens believe Nixon lied to cover up the operation, and almost half of them believe he ordered it in the first place.

CBS interviewer Mike Wallace: *Obviously, the question comes to my mind . . . the father of two little kids like that . . . how can he shoot babies?*

My Lai veteran Paul Meadlo: *I didn't have the little girl. I just had the little boy at the time.*

If one is to understand the new Cuban cinema, one must understand Cuba's absolute identification with Vietnam. Cubans think differently than we do. The advanced military technology of the Pentagon allowed us to wage the longest war in our history at a distance, insulating the collective conscience from the horror. The air war combined with "Vietnamization" reduced U.S. casualties to a minimum, thereby defusing domestic concern, Asian lives meaning little to a nation founded on genocide of Indians, enslavement of Blacks, and war against Mexicans.

The insulation of our sensibilities allowed Michael Schwarz, home after serving a ten-month jail term for the murder of twelve South Vietnamese civilians, to tell his celebrating family, "I'm a professional sniper. I feel that if I go back to Vietnam I could teach other Marines to be snipers while in combat with on-the-job training." It allowed Frank "Red" Walton, a former Los Angeles police officer who once commanded the Watts district, to supervise Saigon's law enforcement and prison techniques, including the infamous Con Son "tiger cages," of which he said, "This place is more like a Boy Scout recreational camp." It allowed former Green Beret Captain Robert Marasco, with the cynicism of one whom nothing surprises, to describe in detail on the Dick Cavett Show just how he had served his country and thereby the audience by assassinating a Vietnamese double agent on orders of the CIA: Yes, two shots in the head; of course after he'd injected the body full of morphine to make the killing humane, then put the body in a mail sack, weighted it with tire irons, dumped the sack into several hundred feet of water in the China Sea, which is shark-infested. The insulation allowed General William Westmoreland, when he oversaw U.S. operations in Indochina, to demand a body count of at least two thousand corpses a week.

Of course it allowed for the slaughter at My Lai, our most public bid for atrocitydom. When veteran Paul Meadlo first broke the story on nationwide television his neighbors had an understanding attitude. "The only thing I blame Paul David for was talking about this to everybody on television," said Dee Henry. "Things like that happen in war. They always have and they always will. It's bad enough to have to kill people without telling everybody about it. This sort of thing should be kept classified." Meadlo had just admitted shooting thirty to forty men, women, and children in the hamlet of My Lai. The babies, he said, might have been holding grenades.

A neighbor of Meadlo, Second Lieutenant Norman Cuttrell, said that in one week he helped destroy thirteen other villages in the Song My area. Colonel Oran Henderson, the highest-ranking officer charged in the crime, said that "Every unit of brigade size has its My Lai hidden some place," but that such incidents remained undisclosed because "every unit doesn't have a Ronald Ridenhour," the Vietnam vet who first disclosed details of the My Lai massacre. Henderson was acquitted, as were the other two officers and two enlisted men brought to trial over the massacre; charges against twelve other officers and seven enlisted men were also dropped. Among the acquittees was Captain Eugene Kotouc, accused of maiming a civilian prisoner whose finger he'd cut off. He said he had no intention of hurting the prisoner when he had the man spread his fingers on a board and made several swiping motions at them with a long knife. Seven career officers on the jury concurred, deliberating less than sixty minutes. Later, at a news conference outside the Fort McPherson courtroom, Kotouc was flushed with excitement and said he would remain in the service. "Who would want to get out of a system like this?" he asked. "It's the best damn Army in the world, I'll tell you." Equally happy was the next My Lai officer exonerated, Captain Thomas Willingham. With his wife at his side, Willingham said his intention now was to return to San Francisco and "try to obtain a job in personnel handling."

Also found not guilty by a military jury of Vietnam battle veterans, this time after sixty-eight minutes of deliberate speed, was Captain Ernest Medina, the commanding officer at the scene of the mass killings. One of the jurors, Colonel Robert Nelson, explained: "We all began this case with the assumption that Captain Medina was innocent and we were waiting for the government to convince us otherwise. I was delighted with the verdict. I hope the adverse publicity the Army has had over the past year and a half will end now." He added that he thought Medina was a fine officer who should stay in the Army. Medina himself was unsure of his future but was immediately offered an executive position by Florida cosmetics millionaire Glenn Turner, who also gave twenty-five thousand dollars to the defense. (Lawyer F. Lee Bailey had helped Turner out of several legal jams in the past.*) Said Turner, "I'm a sucker for causes."

The numerous acquittals and dismissals of charges left First Lieutenant William Calley the only person convicted in the slaughter. Calley's original life sentence was reduced to twenty years and is undergoing review by Commander-in-Chief Nixon, who, in his best Battle of Britain tones, said he would be just. Even so, a Gallup Poll found that 79 per cent of the public disagreed with the guilty verdict in the Calley trial, about a fifth of these arguing that the massacre was not a crime, the rest saying that others were also responsible. According to the Army's charges against him, Calley killed a hundred and two Vietnamese civilians at My Lai. But *Time* magazine reported he had become a celebrity, almost a hero, to some. His secretary collected ten thousand fan letters compared to seven derogatory letters. Said *Time*: "When Calley travels, Delta Air Lines in

* Turner was indicted together with Bailey in the case mentioned above.

Columbus, Georgia, wires ahead to ensure him VIP treatment; recently Delta gave him a first-class seat though he held a coach ticket. When he stops at a bar, Calley invariably finds his drink tab collected by an admirer. While in Washington, when he was undergoing psychiatric tests . . . he had ten dollars thrust at him by a stranger. In Columbus, Calley and his friends are always guests of the house of the Chickasaw Supper Club. A local wine shop gives him a discount. The president of the Fourth National Bank personally expedites Calley's transactions. One day Calley presented his check to a Gatlinburg, Tennessee, bank and the teller said, 'Gee, no kidding, you're Lieutenant Calley?' The check went through immediately." Defenders of Calley perhaps saw in him an extension of themselves: a survey of public attitudes by the Roper organization found that, in response to the question, "What would most people do if ordered to shoot all inhabitants of a Vietnamese village suspected of aiding the enemy, including old men, women, and children?" 67 per cent answered: "Follow orders and shoot." Only 19 per cent said they would not shoot. My Lai had come to be the natural culmination of the American education system among whose most important byproducts are racism and anticommunism.

Lieutenant Calley isn't the only one who made a killing out of My Lai. Ronald Haeberle, a Cleveland businessman assigned to Calley's company at the time of the massacre as a combat photographer, auctioned off eighteen color slides to magazines and newspapers in New York for forty thousand dollars. One magazine editor said, "They must have known they had the hottest private film for sale since Abraham Zapruder asked for bids on his color movies of President Kennedy's assassination." Paul Meadlo was enterprising enough to sell the story of his thirty to forty killings to television for ten thousand dollars. The recording of "Lieutenant Calley's Battle Hymn Marches On" sold 300,000 copies in three days. The massive outburst of support embracing Calley, convicted of multiple premeditated murder, was spontaneous, not organized. The convicted war criminal has been found guilty by his peers of smashing the head of a two-year-old child, among his hundred and two victims. In his defense it was said that he did not feel he was killing humans, only "dinks" or "gooks" or "V.C." In Europe the press made an immediate comparison to Nazi atrocities, in particular the Czech village of Lidice, destroyed in reprisal by the Germans in 1942. But on the day of the Lidice massacre the women and children were spared.

If every brigade had its My Lai, as Colonel Henderson avers, so too did each bomb squadron. A study in *Scientific American* estimates that between 1965 and 1971 the United States dropped 26 billion pounds of explosives in Indochina, twice that used in all theatres of World War II; of that, 21 billion were dropped in South Vietnam, with an area the size of Missouri, creating 21 million craters. The study does not include figures for 1972, the most intensive bombing of any target at any time in history, averaging the equivalent of two Hiroshima-type bombs per week. *New York Times* correspondent Anthony Lewis wrote: "In my generation we grew up believing in America. We knew there was a fundamental decency and humanity in our country. . . . The truth is now impossible to escape if we open our eyes: The United States is the most dangerous and destructive power in the world."

A much-used maxim holds that the guerrilla must be like a fish in the sea of people. But counterrevolution argues that when the sea protects the fish, the sea must be poisoned and dried up. From seeding clouds to increase rainfall, to bombing the centuries-old dike system, to supporting the largest illicit drug traffic in history—American criminality was on a scale without parallel. All of Indochina was a laboratory for experiments in death. U.S. attempts at fire bombing failed only because the jungle foliage was too damp. But military officials suggest that such attempts would be again tried if better methods were devised. What the Pentagon Papers show is that in fact a small number of men sat down and conspired against the peace of the world, planning each day how to destroy a small country on the other side of the globe. The Papers are the prosecution case in another Nuremberg trial.

But the Nuremberg Trials took place because the Reich was defeated on its own territory; Germany was a conquered nation. When the U.S. pulled out of Vietnam it had many more places to "withdraw" to: The Department of Defense property amounts to 202 billion dollars. It owns 39 million acres of land not counting 2,200 foreign bases, rules 4.7 million direct employees or soldiers, spends over 80 billion dollars a year, is contracted to 63 per cent of all U.S. scientists, engineers, and technicians. Much of this power is aimed at making Latin America safe for the International Telegraph and Telephone Company.* In the fifteen years from 1950 to 1965, North American corporations invested 3.8 billion dollars in Latin America, extracting 12 billion dollars profit, an investment worth protecting. Latins could take little comfort when Senator Hugh Scott complained: "The Democrats . . . are desperate to build up Laos as an issue. Why, we have had more casualties in Guatemala than in Laos."

Watergate and Indochina are names from our recent past engraved in the minds of Cuban revolutionaries. Many more since the turn of the century could equally have served to make the point. From the Watergate burglary and our atrocities in the Indochina war, Cubans will conclude that in the United States

---

* Readers who might guess we are here straying far afield should remember the earlier Nixon Administration scandals involving ITT, one of which demonstrated that ITT attempted to have the CIA bring down the legally elected Allende government in Chile, the other showing a $400,000 ITT contribution to Nixon for re-election purposes in exchange for favors. Watergate conspirator E. Howard Hunt was the White House agent dispatched to Colorado to hush up ITT lobbyist Dita Beard at the time.

high crimes are rewarded, not punished, and the highest crimes are committed by the people in highest position. We are constantly told that "communism is only 90 miles away." But for Cubans there is a real worry: the United States is only 90 miles away.

Perhaps because it is an island, revolutionary Cuba is among the most internationalist of countries. It sees itself very much as part of Latin America; as a full partner of the socialist camp; as a sister nation of Vietnam in every sense. Cubans will tell the North American visitor: "Look, your country supported Batista, who tortured and killed 20,000 of our compatriots. Your government has since the beginning of our revolution tried to starve us through economic blockade and armed intervention. For sixty years your governments supported dictatorships in Cuba. Even today you have a military base at Guantánamo as booty from your 'war' with Spain at the end of the last century. This base is unwanted here. So we completely identify with our Vietnamese comrades. What you must understand is that in a very real sense Vietnam is fighting our war for us. Vietnamese blood shed in war with the United States is surrogate Cuban blood. Because if the United States had not been tied down in Indochina, it might very well have tried again to destroy Cuba. And here in Cuba, imperialism could perhaps win. We have no friendly countries on our borders. We have no borders. We have no rearguard retreat and supply areas. We have no allies closer than 10,000 miles away. So you might triumph here, but it would be a Pyrrhic victory in the literal sense. For what the United States would win would be an island of burnt ash and corpses. That is why to understand us you must understand what we think about the United States and about Vietnam."

North American viewers of Cuban films invariably ask why they all have a political connotation. The Cuban movie industry needs no apologia nor defense and the above is not meant to serve as such. Rather it is an explanation of why it is an engaged cinema, constantly revolutionary in substance as well as form.

WAY BACK WHEN

. . . Fifty years ago
In front-page headlines, no less,
The latest baseball news.
How great! Cincinnati beat Pittsburgh.
. . . Modern-minded newspapers
Had a daily page in English for the Yankees:
(A Cuban-American Paper
With the News of the World).
. . . Our memory holds its images captive:
It is simply that we have grown,
We have grown but we don't forget.

Nicolás Guillén,
Poet laureate of Cuba

The development of cinema in Cuba is only part of a major cultural revolution on the island, and cannot be seen separate and apart from the other ninety-nine blooming flowers of the cultural garden. The Cuban Revolution has again demonstrated the bursts of untapped energy and creativity that come when a whole people is mobilized in collective effort. As with public health, where it is the only nation of the Americas to have completely eliminated poliomyelitis, or with athletics, where the teams from this small island completely dominate competition in the hemisphere, so it is with education and culture.

In 1961, Cuba mounted a literacy campaign that sent 270,000 volunteer teachers into the villages and mountains to teach reading and writing to the 25 per cent of Cuba's population that was illiterate. Over a million campesinos and urban dwellers learned to read for the first time in their lives. Among the plethora of impressive statistics of the campaign, one of the more fascinating is that the government gave away free some 177,000 pairs of eyeglasses—remember, these were mainly older learners. When the volunteers came back down out of the mountains, Cuba was the first fully literate nation in the Americas, acclaimed with accolades by the UNESCO team which went two years later to investigate the truth of the claims.

In all of Cuban history before the Revolution, not one million books were published. Now, since the literacy campaign, publishing is a booming industry: 8 million books in 1967, 12 million in 1968, 15 million in 1969, 18 million in 1970, over 20 million in 1971. There are close to a thousand titles in print. Two-thirds of all the books published go into the educational system— primary and secondary schools, universities, correspondence schools, and adult education. Once again, all of these are free to the students. The titles are ecumenical: children's books like *Little Red Riding Hood*, Afro-Cuban poetry, Von Clausewitz on war, Lenin's collected works, García Lorca, letters of Van Gogh, writings of the Guatemalan *guerrillero* Turcios Lima, potboilers by Eric Ambler and Raymond Chandler. The most serious problem in publishing is the shortage of paper. An average first edition is 10,000 books, a figure in itself quite remarkable. In the United States, 5,000 copies is common for a first printing, with a sure best-seller already sold to a book club starting off with 50,000. But an ordinary 10,000 first edition in Cuba is the equivalent, population-wise, of 250,000 in the U.S. Che Guevara's Bolivian diary, given away free to lines that looked like V-E Day on Lower Broadway, was printed in an edition of 500,000 copies. (U.S. equivalent: 12.5 million.) *Portnoy's Complaint* and *The Godfather* combined might sell half of that.

Also following the literacy campaign, a library system developed. For example, Las Villas Province is relatively small, with only six towns of any real size. It had no public library before the Revolution. Now there are thirty-six in all the main centers of the province, and this does not include the public school libraries. Cienfuegos, with its 80,000 citizens, is the second largest town. Its library, opened in 1962, now has about 60,000 volumes.

From the Escambray Mountains to the cities of Havana and Santiago, Cuba has established the most extensive educational system in Latin America. In hundreds of day nurseries, boarding schools, adult education centers, and universities, a whole new society is being raised. All of Batista's old army camps have been turned into huge campuses, as first promised in Fidel Castro's famous "History Will Absolve Me" defense speech in 1953. A typical school-city encompasses one hundred buildings spread over a thousand acres, embracing several thousand primary, secondary, and technical school students and several hundred teachers. They include dormitories, apartments for married teachers, hospitals with dozens of full-time medical and dental staffs. Here are cafeterias, gymnasiums, swimming pools, athletic fields, amphitheaters, and libraries. All the services of a town—telephone, telegraph, post office, stores—are present on campus, without charge. Students receive clothes, shoes, three meals daily, eyeglasses, books, and all other necessities gratis. The cumulative effect of this new education and literacy is a new national personality. One young schoolteacher once told me: "You saw my children this morning, right? Well, those kids really know what the Revolution is about, they really do want 'to be like Che' as a slogan proclaims, they are becoming our first new men and women. You see, we can never be stopped. We have come too far. Every material good may be taken from us and destroyed, but we have revolutionary consciousness and we know what we're about. With that, we can't lose. The world now knows that we are our own people."

The internationalism that the Revolution exudes manifests itself all over the Cuban map: the sugar central named Harlem, the Tamara Bunke Polyclinic, the Camilo Torres school, the Congo Libre Brigade, the sugar central España Republicana, the Fábrica Comuna de Paris, the region Patricio Lumumba, the new school named Los Martires de Kent State. But the main foreign cultural influences are Latin and North American. Prior to the Revolution, U.S. cultural imperialism dominated the island. Commercial culture was geared to the tourist and the sailor in port. Culture, like everything else, was distorted to fill the needs of the *norteamericano*. Even today there are residues of this past, albeit amalgamated with Cuban popular forms, both traditional and newly developed. A visit to the Tropicana night club, on the outskirts of Havana, is a step into a time capsule to emerge onto a 1935 MGM sound stage. The Tropicana, built under the stars amid a landscape of jungle foliage, seats 2,000 diners at three salons. Formerly a mob-run casino, with George Raft fronting, much of the entertainment hasn't changed. Here is a Carmen Miranda singer, there a Jerry Colonna comic, here a Veloz and Yolanda dance team, there a spangle-suited pianist on a sliding spiral staircase playing a polonaise. This is the stuff which used to provide Ed Sullivan with his bread and butter: everything but the motorcyclist through the hoop of fire. The men all asplendor in white bucks, string ties, and cummerbunds, the women with their beehive and bouffant wigs and rhinestone-speckled dresses. Mascara and pomade abound. The star singer wears a dress whose material contains a relief of velvet, like the wallpaper at a Tad's $1.95 Steak House. At the revue's climax, a seven-layer waterfall descends as backdrop, with different colored lights trained upon it; now scarlet and turquoise, now azure and silver. But the climax of the show is an Afro-Cuban ensemble, developed by the Academy of Science in an attempt to recapture the native culture suppressed and distorted by the former U.S. presence. When the show ends, sudden shoots of steam and water surround the nightclub, a thousand geysers with colors changing like Mulholland fountain in Los Angeles. Finally come the ten thousand lights blinking on and off, forming stars, the Cuban flag, revolutionary slogans and other patterns: it is Vegas's Golden Nugget, Forty-second Street's Fascination, and the Joshua Light Show.

Prerevolutionary U.S. influences are becoming historical museum pieces. A major scene in revolutionary Cuba's best-known novel and screenplay in the West, Edmundo Desnoes' *Memories of Underdevelopment* (*Memorias del Subdesarrollo*), takes place in the old Hemingway estate. Now El Museo Hemingway, the old man's house and gardens were given to the Revolution by the writer's widow. The mansion is located above the village of San Francisco, a cluster of one-room wooden shacks; the last shack on the road leading to the Hemingway grounds houses the local Committee for the Defense of the Revolution. To approach the house, one winds his way up past the swimming pool and through all the foliage covering his several lawns. Ernesto was obviously an eccentric. The dozen rooms are maintained exactly as Hemingway left them, down to the last unfinished bottle and the last unopened *Sports Illustrated*. Lining the walls of every room, bathroom included, are what might be the local branch public library. Several thousand volumes, all in English. Above the bookshelves are the mounted heads of a seeming herd of African wildlife, victims of the Great Man's hunting prowess. There are a dozen lions, possibly three times that many antelopes, deer, and brethren. Not all the animal life in the joint has gone to the Great Safari in the Sky. Hemingway maintained a virtual menagerie of cats—over fifty of them. About ten yards from the house is a three-story tower-like structure consisting of one twelve-by-twelve room on each floor, built by his wife as a gift to Ernest to house his trophies on one floor, store his hunting, fishing, and skiing equipment on another. The top floor was to serve as a retreat, where he could be alone in peace. After fifteen minutes in the room, the quiet was so unnerving he couldn't write a word, so he carried his typewriter back to the big house, never to return to his new digs. Instead he turned the three floors into a literal cat house, letting his assorted and sundry felines have the run of the place. The guide remarks that Hemingway was a good man, a humane man, a friend of the Revolution, but no revolutionary. His servants should testify to the latter evaluation. He was not only a good writer but a rich writer. The museum guide says that Hemingway always came to this Cuban house when he had a problem to solve. One is quick to think of his last problem, whose final solution came at his Idaho ranch home.

What is so striking is the amalgam of the new Cuba—with its attempt to recapture the battered traditions—and the lingering North American influences from *before 1960*. Washington's economic blockade against Cuba has resulted in a peculiar phenomenon: The only U.S. cultural penetration is fifteen years old or more. Which has served Cuba by allowing it to proceed to make its revolution in its own style.

> *Cuba is a socialist country: tropical, unpolished, ingenuous, and gay. It is socialist, without relinquishing even one of its own characteristics while it adds to its people's maturity. It is worth getting acquainted with.*
>
> Ernesto Che Guevara

To speak of Cuban cinema is to speak of revolutionary Cuban cinema. There just wasn't a Cuban film industry, properly speaking, before the Revolution came to power. The island was a source of cheap tropical locations for Hollywood studios; there was a poorly equipped dubbing studio to help Cubans enjoy North American film fare; the Batista dictatorship allowed some amateurish self-serving newsreels to proclaim its good deeds, which turned out to be as stirring as the history of Greenland; and of course some of the more famous porno flicks of their time were made there. The theatre circuit, for the most part limited to the cities, was controlled by U.S. chains, with some inroads into the interior made by the even more grossly commercial Mexican cinema. Every now and then attempts were made at film making by Cubans, but these were shoddy imitations of already shoddy imports, and failed commercially.

In the course of the armed struggle against the dictatorship, a few protest documentaries and newsreels were made by revolutionaries in the Sierra and the urban underground. Again, these were of the barest cinematic qualities. One of these film makers, a former student federation leader and schoolmate of Fidel Castro, was Alfredo Guevara. With the triumph of the Revolution, Guevara became an administrative assistant to Fidel. Several weeks after the *barbudos* (bearded ones) entered Havana, Castro called Guevara to ask that he prepare a law founding the Cuban Film Institute. On March 24, 1959, the law was proclaimed, the first law in the field of culture by the Revolution.

The ICAIC (Instituto Cubano del Arte e Industria Cinematograficos) serves, in the Cuban order of things, as something of a Ministry of Film. It oversees all aspects of the budding film industry: the training of film students; the production of newsreels, documentaries, and features; the supervision of Cuban theatres; the import and export films.

Guevara has said that a major effort of the ICAIC goes to educate Cuban audiences as to the nature of film. For those who were film-goers before the Revolution, their taste was corrupted by the Hollywood and Mexican fare. "This is a public," he says, "that still looks for this kind of product, that feels lost without it, even though it knows better politically. . . . If we don't educate this public to understand nuances, educate them to the full significance of the political, social, and historical problems of the treatment of the characters, we will always have that open window—and . . . people desperate to get through it. People do not enjoy and accept such cinema because of the ideology it

transmits, but because it comes wrapped in language understandable to them." This is a problem Cuban productions will
overcome in time but which meanwhile cannot be avoided. To
deal with it, ICAIC continues to import entertainment films
(among Cuban favorites are Japanese Samurai and Soviet spy
movies) and also those of a political nature. Emphasis in
publicity, on balance, is given to the political film. Also, the
Cuban audience prefers to hear a film in Spanish, so that
Vietnamese films, often rudimentary and made under the most
trying of conditions, are dubbed in Spanish to make them more
attractive. The great Cuban revolutionary art form, together
with film, is the poster, and many of Cuba's best poster artists
are attached to ICAIC, which uses this graphic talent to spur
attendance.

More important than serving the pre-Revolution audience, in
ICAIC's perspective, is taking the cinema to the peasantry. Says
Guevara, "This is an area of the public that is very interesting;
precisely because it did not know the old commercial cinema,
it is not warped. It is warped in another way, however, because
ignorance is warping. So our efforts have been concentrated on
this public and in the areas where the cinema was once unknown,
we now have 13 million moviegoers a year." ICAIC runs the
500 theatres that dot the island, but has developed other
methods for reaching the more remote areas of the countryside
and mountains. Redesigned trucks, equipped with 16-mm.
projectors and driven by projectionists, spread out across the
country to show films in those areas where there are not yet
theatres. These *cines moviles* now number more than a hundred.
One of ICAIC's most engaging short documentaries, *Por Primera
Vez* (*For the First Time*), is actually about this part of the
ICAIC operation: the episode photographed shows one evening
when a projection crew went to an area in the Baracoa section
of the Sierra to show a film to people there "*por primera vez*"—
the film: Chaplin's *Modern Times*. In interviews with *guajiras*

before the film is shown, they are asked what they think a film is. One replies: "I haven't seen one but I think it might be a party or a dance or something like that. . . . What I do want is to see it so that nobody can tell me what it is." Most of the prize-winning short simply trains the camera on the uninitiated audience with joyful results.

The attempt to demystify the cinema for an audience of novices is more than a little difficult to understand for a North American, whose sensibilities are bombarded to numbness by the electronic media. ICAIC has set itself the task of bringing young people interested in the cinema into discussion circles at student centers, union halls, and workplaces to explain its work. More important, it seeks to explain the methods of film to the entire population, to work in a way against its own power, according to Guevara, "to reveal all the tricks, all the recourses of language, to dismantle all the mechanisms of cinematographic hypnosis." To this end, ICAIC has a weekly television program which explains all the gimmicks used to attract the viewer's attention.

When it began, ICAIC used the most elementary techniques. Most of the film workers were uneducated in the media, although a handful had studied in European film schools. Today, with a number of fully developed cadres, the acquisition of skills is now a secondary concern at best. Guevara explains that the priority is to "break down the bourgeois language," being very careful in the process not to divorce the film maker from the audience for the film maker's own self-gratification. Guevara puts it this way: "We must not separate ourselves from the rest of the people, from all the tasks of the Revolution, especially those that fall into the ideological field. Every time a school is built, every time 100 workers reach the sixth grade, each time someone discovers something by participating in it, as in the field of culture, it becomes easier to make our work real and not an illusion. Our work is not simply making or showing movies: everything we do is part of a global process toward developing the possibilities of participation—not passive but active, not as recipients but as protagonists of the public." That is the Cuban definition of socialist democracy in the field of culture.

A North American at a Cuban theatre finds that the audience is half the show: Movies are an audience-participation game, much as is a baseball game. People catcall, applaud or derogate, offer advice—serious or facetious—to the screen images, wisecrack for the benefit of spectators in the immediate vicinity, and call to friends a couple of rows away. It is a bit like a Loew's Saturday matinee and, on a more raucous day, reaches for comparison with Shea Stadium.

U.S. films shown in Cuba are of course from the pre-Revolution period: *Gigi*, *Singing in the Rain*, *Bad Day at Black Rock*. Late-night television repeats from time to time a Dana Andrews or Ronald Coleman melodrama. The economic blockade against Cuba has denied the island access to U.S. movies of the sixties and seventies, though from time to time a bootleg print gets through. A recent favorite there was *The Chase* with Marlon Brando and Jane Fonda, from the early sixties. Imports are in large part from the European socialist countries, France, Italy, Japan, and Latin America. Cuban taste is fairly catholic: audience favorites range from the French *Umbrellas of Cherbourg* to Soviet anti-Nazi spy films to the Brazilian *Antonio Das Mortes* to the Italian-Algerian *Battle of Algiers*. All imports are limited by the shortage of hard currency for bartering on the international market.

Obviously the shortage of currency is a great burden for ICAIC's production department as well. To this day, the Institute does not own even one super-8 camera. There are no color facilities in Cuba, though a lab is now under construction. Consequently, with *Days of Water (Los Días del Agua)*, Cuba's first color feature film, the director could not see rushes as he filmed. He had to wait two and three weeks for the film to be sent to Spain, developed, and returned before he could screen the material. Alfredo Guevara says, "Even when we have had the resources, we have had to solve problems of extreme urgency. In this country there were millions of peasants who never saw movies and we have sometimes preferred to buy trucks and equipment for those trucks than new camera equipment." Outside of Cuba, ICAIC's documentary shorts and *noticieros* are perhaps its best-known product. These dazzling films, under the supervision of Santiago Alvarez, are again the result of making the most of limited resources. Alvarez's brilliant free-wheeling editing (which at one point moved Godard to call him the world's best documentarian) often are montages of still photos, *Life* covers, pen-and-ink cartoons; Western news footage just isn't available to Cuba, and Cuban newsmen are barred from the United States, the inspiration for a good many Alvarez productions.

Even given its financial handicaps and only twelve years of operation, Cuba has been able to develop a major national cinema, the *premiere* cinema of Latin America. This comes as a bit of a surprise to many Westerners (in the United States, moviegoers remain in complete ignorance of Cuban film, leading some to suspect that the U.S. blockade is in part aimed at its own citizenry), but is partially explained by the cohesiveness of ICAIC and its overall relationship to the Cuban Revolution. Its organization of collective energies, its revolutionary will to go where the more angelic fear to tread, its self-image as a weapon in a larger struggle rather than an isolated end unto itself—these are what make for ICAIC's success. From the beginning, ICAIC has been faced with a dialectic contradiction: it wants to capture for posterity and for the moment the complex reality of these years, but the reality is always changing. Alfredo Guevara says: "They are surely the most difficult, the most complicated years, years in which the experiences we have are sometimes not recorded. To reflect them in the cinema means that in some way we must crystallize them, which is the last thing we want. But every time we film, it is there. Whether or not we want to do so, we're always a testimony."

The poster commemorating the tenth anniversary of ICAIC shows a camera with gunsmoke exuding from the lens. The imagery of film maker as cultural *guerrillero* corresponds to the value system throughout revolutionary Cuba. Guevara says: "With the success of the Revolution, we had placed in our hands a thing (the means of communication) whose power we knew very well because it had been the power of the enemy up to that point. When this force fell into our hands, it was clear to all of us that the Revolution had given us a very serious job. I'm talking . . . of everyone who has participated in the work of giving birth to the Cuban cinema or, what is really the same thing, the job of giving our people and our Revolution a new weapon, a new instrument of work, one that is useful, above all, in understanding ourselves."

A constant theme of the Cuban Revolution is the elimination of distinctions within the population, the unity of the whole people. The United States being closer to the island than New York is to Philadelphia goes a long way in helping develop this theme. Continual efforts are made to reduce distinctions between worker and intellectual, to create worker-intellectuals, and intellectual workers; between town and countryside; between leadership and citizenry; between young and old. Other helping factors in making this effort—factors absent in most of Latin America—are a Catholic Church without great influence, and a relative absence of national minority distinctions. If there is a problem for the Revolution, and for ICAIC, it is in explaining to those too young to remember what Cuba was like before the Revolution. The militance of the present generations is secure: it is sustained in the memory of and struggle against the time when millions were starving, unemployed, uneducated, and without hope; when Cuba belonged to another country which used it as a brothel and playground. But Cuban children have no memory of that period of struggle. For them ICAIC must re-create the past. (A curious phenomenon has arisen in recent Western cinema: the attempt to recapture, in however commercial and distorted a manner, the radical history of the United States. Three of the great stories of our radical past—Sacco and Vanzetti, the Molly McGuires, and Joe Hill—have been filmed by *European* film makers. So far, no American—commercial or "underground"—has explored this history. Which speaks to the question of what makes Cuban film revolutionary and North American—even "revolutionary"—cinema not: a revolution is a culmination of a process and not an instant formula. To deny one's past is to deny an understanding of what is present.)

Since José Marti, the Cuban patriot and writer, Cuba has identified as an immutable part of Latin America. But Latin America today—with police torture, illiteracy, hunger, low life expectancy and high infant mortality—provides young Cubans with a mirror on their nation's past. Thus the ICAIC emphasis on Latin American subjects. Guevara argues, "It is terrible to see the most horrible misery coexisting with opulence. In that kind of situation we see the image of everything that remains to be liberated, we see the context in which the revolutionary struggle takes place. That is why we all feel that the Cuban cinema not be 'Cuban' cinema but that it be a cinema directed toward Latin America. We believe that is the way to make the most 'Cuban' cinema. We have always wanted this to be the basic starting point of our work, Latin Americans speaking to Latin Americans. We do not direct ourselves only to a society that is building socialism but also to a continent that fights for liberation as well as socialism." It is the same concern that else-where in the cultural field makes Casa de las Americas the most prestigious publishing house in Cuba; and that in the political field led Che Guevara to make his heroic sacrifice. It is interesting, in this context, to note that most North Americans who have seen Cuban films (a limited number certainly) prefer as a favorite *Memories of Underdevelopment*, perhaps the least "Cuban" film ICAIC has produced. Critics judge it "better than the early Antonioni" and liken its lead actor, Sergio Corrieri, to Marcello Mastroianni, as it traces the career of a *petit bourgeois* who is paralyzed in his attempt to adjust to the Revolution, while his family has left him for the United States.

ICAIC's desire not to "crystallize" the present complexities on celluloid, combined with the parallel goal of creating a "Latin" cinema to identify Cuba with the whole continent in its misery and its struggle to overcome, may go some distance toward explaining the fact that Cuban feature films treat historical themes more often than not, leaving contemporary subjects to the documentaries. (Some critics of the Revolution argue that feature-film makers want to play it safe, to avoid possible reprisals for inaccurate representations of current events.) The ICAIC direction is in any case basically documentary, spontaneity and the dynamic of the moment being the essence of the Cuban tendency. "This is reflected even in the fictional movie," says Guevara, "because since we do not consider them to be different things, but only different ways to express the same reality, directors often work on a fiction film one day, on a documentary the next, and then later return to the fiction film. Two things are reflected, two genres that have a false boundary placed between them, imposed by a commercial exploitation. In our fiction film, there is a lot of documentary."

Documentary footage, for example, of counterrevolutionary violence in Havana and of President Kennedy's missile-crisis address are inserted into the feature *Memories of Underdevelopment*. *The First Charge of the Machete*, about Cuba's first war of independence in the mid-nineteenth century, fuses documentary hand-held camera work and news interviewing techniques to simulate early news footage. Conversely, Cuban documentary films are often feature-length, as with the major work on Indochina, *Third World, Third World War*. And the shorts rely on music and pictures to the exclusion of narration, as with *79 Springtimes*, a lyric tribute to the life of Ho Chi Minh; *Take-off at 18:00*, which compares Cuba's mass mobilization to eliminate underdevelopment with a military struggle; and *Cyclone*, about the devastating effects of a Caribbean hurricane. Perhaps being a new cinema, that has come of age in an era of unprecedented technological as well as political-economic revolution, has also forged this unique documentary characteristic on Cuban film. A similiar, though unrelated, phenomenon is true of U.S. creative writing, in which the best novelists of our country find their highest expression in journalism and essays: Mailer, Baldwin, Algren, Bourjailly, Capote, etc.

In any case, ICAIC has produced some 50 medium- to full-length feature films since 1959, perhaps 300 documentary shorts, and close to 500 *noticieros*. This outburst of creativity has reaped for Cuba a harvest of laurels and prizes at numerous film festivals in Latin America, Asia, and Europe. Only North Americans, among major audiences for film, have been denied the opportunity to view the Cuban cinema.

> *Gee, but I want to be a G-Man*
> *And go bung bung bung bung bung.*
> Song from 1930s musical,
> "Pins & Needles"

When U.S. crematoria in the form of B-52's were incinerating babies in Asia, and little-more-than-babies are shooting heroin in the U.S., it seems almost incidental that a cultural event like the first U.S. Festival of Cuban Films was halted by the government. But incidental it isn't.

The Festival was announced in December 1971 to take place at New York City's Olympia Theatre from March 24 through

April 2, 1972. The seven feature films and fifteen documentaries to be shown had received unanimous critical acclaim and favorable audience response from Lima, Peru, to Leipzig, Germany. All of the films had received prizes at leading film festivals in Europe, Asia, and Latin America. The Festival itself, as a package, had been exhibited the year before at London's National Film Theatre under the auspices of the British Film Institute, a government-supported group in that country. The film critic for *The New York Times* said that the Festival promised to be "the most important film retrospective of the year." Only one element in the Festival stood in the way of this becoming an outstanding success by U.S. standards: these important films were produced in revolutionary Cuba.

American Documentary Films (ADF), a nonprofit media organization with offices in San Francisco and New York, proposed to ICAIC in 1971 the idea of having a Festival in New York and other U.S. cities. ADF had for a few years distributed to schools, churches, and community groups in the United States 16-mm. documentaries from Cuba, as well as dozens of socially critical films dealing with poverty, the economy, Black liberation, and Indochina.

As a result of Washington's embargo against Cuba, the people of the United States have not been allowed to enjoy the new revolutionary culture of Cuba. The dance critic of *The New York Times* has, for example, had to travel to Montreal to rave about the Cuban Ballet. Obviously there would be some public opposition to the Festival and the government would not take a liking to it, but ADF proceeded to promote it in the knowledge that it was within its rights to do so. The first announcement of the Festival came at a December press conference at the Museum of Modern Art, which was to host a Cuban Film Day as its part of the ten-day event. The press conference also announced that invitations had been issued to Cuban film makers to be present at the Festival. Such invitations are a matter of course for film festivals, whether they be at Cannes or Tashkent. But this was New York and these were Cubans.

On January 13, 1972, the Cuban film makers—Alfredo Guevara, Santiago Alvarez, Jorge Fraga, and Saul Yelin— applied for visas, through the Czechoslovakian Embassy in Washington, which handles Cuban affairs in the U.S. in the absence of state relations between the two countries. Meanwhile several university film schools—NYU, Yale, Antioch—the Museum of Modern Art, television station WNET, and others also invited the Cubans to participate in various seminars and discussions on film. Support for the visas came from numerous film personalities and critics, including Otto Preminger, Vincent Canby, Ossie Davis, Geraldine Page, Faye Dunaway, Jane Fonda, Jules Feiffer, Richard Schickel, Arthur Miller, Ruby Dee, Burgess Meredith, Norman Mailer, Rip Torn, John Lennon, and many others.

In the third week of February 1972, the First Lady and the President were in Peking, China. At a state banquet, Pat allowed as how she had eaten Chinese food all over the world but nowhere had it been as good as here in China. The President raised his glass and toasted: "Chairman Mao has written: 'So many deeds cry out to be done, and always urgently. The world rolls on. Time passes. Ten thousand years are too long. Seize the day.' Seize the hour. This is the hour. This is the day for our two peoples to rise to the heights of greatness which can build a new and a better world. And in that spirit I ask all of you present to join me in raising your glasses to Chairman Mao, to Prime Minister Chou, and to the friendship of the Chinese and American people, which can lead to friendship and peace for all people in the world." On that day, the U.S. State Department denied the visas to the Cubans. No reason for the denial was given in the curt note to the Czech Embassy, but visa section chief James E. Kiley said the rejection came for "national security" reasons. Which prompted Senate Foreign

Relations Committee Chairman J. William Fulbright to inquire why the U.S. government should consider four film makers a security threat and not Mao Tse-tung and the People's Republic of China. Among other protestors were Senators Edward Kennedy and George McGovern, Mayor John Lindsay, the New York *Post*, and the Los Angeles *Times*.

In March President Nixon, back from China, vacationed with exiled Cuban banker Bebe Rebozo in his Key Biscayne, Florida, residence. At the Sonesta Beach Hotel, down the coast, the Grand Cuban Costume Ball was held. "This ball, which we hope will be an annual affair, is the continuation of the Red Ball of the Country Club of Havana," said Mrs. Gregorio Escagedo, the beneficiary. (The Havana Country Club in its time was so racist that President Batista was barred because he was mulatto. The Country Club is now the site of revolutionary Cuba's National School of Art.) Another bejeweled exile exclaimed: "This is Cuba. Everybody who is anybody in the Cuban society is here." But meanwhile in New York, new attacks began against ADF. While the ball was rolling in Key Biscayne, shotgun blasts were fired through ADF's office windows. The police investigated but said nothing could be done to prevent a recurrence. The next evening a rock barrage again smashed the newly replaced windows. Again the police claimed helplessness. For a week, articles and editorials in the right-wing Spanish-language press had promised that "blood would run in the streets" if "Castroist spies" were allowed to proceed with the Festival. After the shotgun and rock attacks, a manifesto was published claiming credit for the vigilante actions by a group calling itself the "Cuban Liberation Army," which apparently intended to "liberate" Cuba by beginning with Manhattan's Upper West Side.

Then attacks began on the Olympia Theatre which was to house the Festival. Its all-glass façade and box office were destroyed by rocks one night. The next night two fire bombs were set in the theatre but caught before damage could be done. Telegrams were dispatched to the Mayor demanding protection and holding the city responsible for further damage to persons or property. The Mayor, at the time a candidate for the Democratic presidential nomination, was reached through his campaign headquarters and appealed to on the basis that various liberal Democrats were speaking up and he wouldn't want to be outflanked within his own party; and that numerous United Nations diplomats were expected to attend the Festival and he didn't want an international scandal on his hands. Immediately thereafter, the Chief of Police for Manhattan North and a dozen others from Intelligence and other sections came into the case. A security force—including several friendly Cuban exiles—was organized by the Festival Committee to protect the theatre. No more violence was forthcoming, although bomb threats were made sporadically.

Shortly after these incidents, U.S. Treasury agent Eli Slotkin visited the ADF New York office in what was to begin the largest attack on the Festival. ADF spokesmen declined to answer Slotkin's questions until an appointment could be arranged between Slotkin and the film group's attorney. After consultation with the attorney, meanwhile, ADF applied to the Federal Reserve Bank for an import license for the films, transported from Canada several months earlier. When Slotkin and the lawyer met, Slotkin was informed that the license was applied for and pending. Festival coordinators agreed to answer, on attorney's advice, all questions put by the government. Answering in detail, they made one exception, also on attorney's advice: they declined to say who the Canadian source was from whom the films were received. The day before the Festival opened, March 23, ADF received in the morning a letter from the Federal Reserve Bank to the effect that its license was pending and requesting detailed answers to questions within thirty days. Later that same day, Slotkin and customs agent Clarence Barnes showed up at ADF headquarters to demand the films be turned over. On legal advice—the agents had no warrants—the request was denied. That evening another bomb threat was received.

Despite the varied forms of harassment, official and vigilante, the Festival opened on Friday the twenty-fourth to an overflow crowd, including diplomats from twenty-two missions to the United Nations. Press reports the next day gave most play to a couple of white mice released during the performance by right-wing Cuban exiles, causing a disturbance that took some five minutes to dispose of. Two weeks earlier, the premiere of *The Godfather* was attended, appropriately enough, by Henry Kissinger, to great publicity by the press corps. Yet the premiere of the Cuban Film Festival drew more attention to two white mice than to the twenty-two ambassadors.

The next day, after the diplomats had gone home, and just prior to the matinee screening of *Days of Water*, agents Slotkin and Barnes, looking like day-old coffee tastes, raided the theatre and seized the prize-winning film. A subsequent raid of ADF offices three hours later, in an attempt to confiscate the other two dozen films, brought only frustration to the G-men. The films had been removed long before for safekeeping. Nicholas von Hoffman, the Washington *Post* syndicated columnist, likened the Slotkin-Barnes raid to the Izzy and Moe prohibition era revenoors popping out of the ground to knock over speak-easies, only this time going after a neighborhood moviehouse. Neither the Treasury Department nor any other branch of the federal government was pursuing with equal vigor the International Telephone and Telegraph Company, which that month had been shown to pay off the Republican Party in return for favors in antitrust suits, as well as conspiring to overthrow the constitutional government of Chile.

The seizure of the film that day and subsequent raids on ADF's New York and San Francisco offices halted the First U.S. Festival of Cuban Films. The Museum of Modern Art was forced to cancel its Cuban Film Day when Treasury officials falsely told it that it would be committing a criminal action, a threat which those officials subsequently denied. The American Film Institute in Washington, D.C., also canceled the Festival, which it had booked for several days following the New York opening, for fear of running into the federal government, which supplies much of its funds.* Agent Slotkin at one point indicated, off the record, that ADF had put Treasury in a bind: it was one thing to show a 15-minute 16-mm. Cuban short to Kansas State Teachers Normal every now and then; but when you have U.S. Senators speaking on your behalf, and large-scale advertising in the New York metropolitan press, and films booked into the American Film Institute with congressmen invited to the screening, well then, you are breaking the blockade and have to be stopped.†

ADF argued that it had gone out of its way to show good faith. It had offered to swear affidavits in language of the government's choosing to the effect that it had never and hadn't at the time given money to Cuba. It had opened its books, records, correspondence, and several hundred documents to the Treasury Department. Still the license was not granted, because the government claimed that it could never be sure of ADF's innocence. The entire course of U.S. jurisprudence was being

* The American Film Institute was again involved a year later (April 1973) in a similar though unrelated piece of censorship. On the eve of an AFI fundraising benefit honoring John Ford, at which President Nixon was the special guest, the Institute canceled its own premiere of Costa-Gavras's *State of Siege*, a film showing U.S.-aided police torture in Latin America.

† Through a bureaucratic idiosyncrasy, the Treasury Department considers the news media exempt from its foreign assets regulations. Hence the print of *Memories of Underdevelopment* that was to be shown at the Cuban Film Festival was brought into the United States a year earlier by a newsman who declared it important for his work. Later, in answer to the ADF suit against the Treasury Department for its license, the government stipulated that this print of *Memories of Underdevelopment* was acceptable for showing inside the U.S. In May 1973 the film opened commercially in New York to rave reviews. See p. 44.

reversed as the burden of proof and assumption of guilt were both on ADF. The then Attorney General, John Mitchell, had a few months before complained that the courts had a "preoccupation with fairness for the accused," an obviously un-American obsession. At an FBI Academy ceremony, Mitchell was named by the late J. Edgar Hoover as "a special agent of the FBI." Complained Mitchell: "A wave of legalisms has descended on our criminal justice system. Every conceivable twisting and turning is used to weight the side of the defendant."* In the Cuban film caper, ADF was *ipso facto* the culprit, reminding one of Churchill's remark about an antagonist of his: "He always played the game. And he always lost."

A meeting between a Festival spokesman and Stanley Sommerfield, Acting Head of Foreign Assets Control in Washington, was straight out of *Catch-22*. Sure, said Sommerfield, the government exempts the news media and universities from the Cuban embargo statutes because news gathering and a body of scholarship are in the national interest. But no, he continued in answer to a question, it would not be in the national interest if the population as a whole had direct access to the materials instead of having selected elites act as middlemen in deciphering them; that would be breaking the embargo. The Treasury Department would not give ADF a license because ADF had not given him all the facts. Yes, he admitted, the only fact he hadn't been given was the name of the party in Montreal. But if ADF gave him this fact he still couldn't give the license. Why? Because Treasury still didn't have all the facts. A circle without end or beginning. Nicholas von Hoffman wrote in his Washington *Post* column: "Go every morning to your hutch in the Treasury

---

* It will be curious to see if defendant Mitchell reverses this earlier position of prosecutor Mitchell. Already Henry Kissinger, himself an admitted wiretapper against his own staff, has called for "compassion" for the Watergate conspirators, leading some to wonder if he will next ask for amnesty.

Department, Mr. Sommerfield, drink your coffee, read your paper, and daily bring a full measure of aggravation into the lives of people who don't yet know your name. Keep out the movies. . . . The rest of the Treasury Department will let the heroin flow in."

Many critics of the government, including von Hoffman, blamed Foreign Assets Control's actions on absurd bureaucratic extremes, and there were some elements of this involved. But the major factor is the vindictive and antiquated imperialist stance of the United States towards Cuba. The President could exchange musk oxen for Chinese pandas but ADF couldn't show Cuban films on a no-exchange basis. The so-called new Nixon was still the cold warrior who initiated the mercenary invasion at the Bay of Pigs. What began as, and was meant to be, a cultural event was made a political issue by the U.S. government. The one hopeful sign perhaps is that the Administration is taking seriously the argument that culture is a weapon.

Virtually every important film critic in the New York area protested the government's repression of the Festival: Vincent Canby of the *Times*, Jay Cocks of *Time* magazine, Stanley Kauffmann, Dwight Macdonald, Jonas Mekas, Andrew Sarris, Amos Vogel, William Wolfe of *Cue*. Two lawsuits were filed against the State and Treasury Departments, respectively, by lawyers of the National Emergency Civil Liberties Committee. Both called for injunctions against withholding the visas and the license. ADF complained that clearly, protestations to the contrary notwithstanding, the government was trying to repress the Festival: first it stopped the film makers from entering the country, then it stopped the films. Co-plaintiffs in the two suits included Vincent Canby, television executive Jack Willis, Michael Webb of the American Film Institute, Professor Theodore Perry of the NYU film school, Thomas Quigley of the U.S. Catholic Conference, the congress of Catholic bishops in this country, and film makers and critics Susan Sontag, Dwight Macdonald, and Lee Lockwood.

A host of congressmen also spoke to the issues, among them Senators Fulbright, Hughes, Kennedy, McGovern, and Bayh. In a congressional speech, Fulbright argued: "I find it passing strange that the Treasury Department would be so terrified of the impact of Cuban films on the American people, while the State Department is encouraging such exchanges with the Soviet Union." Part of the government's rationale for the continued embargo against Cuba is that the latter country maintains military ties with the USSR, which Fulbright found ironic since obviously the USSR therefore maintained ties with Cuba and this didn't affect our cultural relations with Moscow. "One can only conclude," said the Arkansas Senator, "that the real basis for administration policy lies in the fact that the Soviet Union is a big strong country that we have to get along with, while Cuba is a small weak country that we can afford to kick around. This may be good geopolitics, but it is not a very smart foreign policy, especially in view of the fact that most countries in the world are small and weak, and in view of the further fact that bullies do not have very good track records for distance."

Two weeks after the United States government closed down the first U.S. Festival of Cuban Films in the spring of 1972, the *Wall Street Journal* reported that the Nixon Administration had ordered U.S. warships in the Caribbean to intervene should the Cuban navy attempt to seize private vessels. (Since Playa Girón, exile groups, and CIA mercenaries use private ships to run raids along the Cuban coast or for surveillance.) Air Force jets are ordered to scramble to the scene and U.S. commanders are authorized to "continue interposing until further Cuban aggression creates a situation of self-defense for U.S. forces."

In the fall of 1972, the Supreme Court upheld a lower court ruling barring Belgian economist Ernest Mandel from entering the United States because of his leftist political beliefs. The ruling negated ADF's suit against the State Department on behalf of the Cuban film makers. Earlier a New York judge ruled that the ADF suit against the Treasury Department should go to trial. Because of financial and other considerations ADF was unable to go to trial. In November, American Documentary Films, Inc., of New York declared bankruptcy. The tens of thousands of dollars lost through the suppression of the Cuban Film Festival was the final economic blow to the small radical film group operating in corporate America.

Michael Myerson
March 1973

Memories of
Underdevelopment

(1968)

About
Memories
of Underdevelopment

The Guatemalan guerrilla-poet Otto René Castillo wrote, shortly
before his death, in the poem "Apolitical Intellectuals":

> No one will ask them
> about their dress,
> their long siestas
> after lunch,
> no one will want to know
> about their sterile combats
> with "the idea
> of the nothing"
> no one will care about
> their higher financial learning.
> They won't be questioned
> on Greek mythology,

or regarding their self-disgust
when someone within them
begins to die
the coward's death.
They'll be asked nothing
about their absurd
justifications,
born in the shadow
of the total lie. . . .

A vulture of silence
will eat your gut.
Your own misery
will pick at your soul.
And you will be mute
                    in your shame.

The thing about revolutionary film makers, about Cuban film makers, is that they don't have the luxury of making apolitical movies. Survival negates self-indulgence. The actual political-economic situation negates metaphysics.

Marxists believe that hitherto recorded history is the history of class struggle; that the main class contradiction of our epoch is that between the working class and the capitalist class; that on a world scale that contradiction takes the form of the struggle between the socialist states (where the working class has taken power) and the imperialist states. There may be individual *bourgeois* who are able to reject their class interests as there may be individual workers who strive to become part of the *bourgeoisie*. But Marxist analysis deals primarily with class interests, not individual pursuits. The middle class, the *petit bourgeoisie*, is squeezed out in the course of sharpened class struggle. Composed of small businessmen, professionals, and intellectuals, this stratum (as Marxists see it) is constantly vacil-

lating. It has the option of aligning itself with, and serving, either class.

Not to grasp this concept is to deny an understanding of Tomás Gutiérrez Alea's *Memories of Underdevelopment* (1968). Most Western critics have compared the film to early Antonioni, its star Sergio Corrieri to the young Mastroianni, and their portrayals of the middle class alienated in the vapidness of modern Italian society. But revolutionary Cuba is not capitalist Italy, and the milieu in which Corrieri's Sergio operates (or, rather, cannot operate) is far different from that pictured by Antonioni. Some European and North American writers, to make their point, have made much of the fact that Gutiérrez Alea (shown above) studied film in Italy, and screenwriter Edmundo Desnoes (the screenplay is an adaptation of his novel of the same name*) spent several years in New York. The fact however is that they

* Published in the United States as *Inconsolable Memories*, New York: New American Library, 1967.

returned to Cuba to help make the Revolution. Desnoes has recently served on the staff of the Communist Party's educational-propaganda agency, much to the dismay of some North American intellectuals who upon being misinformed that he was an "imprisoned dissident" of the Revolution at one time rushed to embrace his "cause."

The film, in any case, is remarkable, as noted by virtually every critic of the medium. *New York Times* critic Vincent Canby wrote, "It remains a lovely achievement, one of the finest Latin American films to be seen in New York (no matter how briefly) in the last 12 years." Canby added in a later review, "The result is hugely effective and moving, and it is complete in the way that very few movies ever are." Penelope Gilliatt in *The New Yorker* calls *Memories* "a beautifully organized picture in its technique, with the most skillful possible use of voice-over, of newsreel footage of the Bay of Pigs, and of leaps backward and forward in time. The note is sardonic and also immensely affectionate toward effort. It is a startling combination in a film made in a revolutionary country. . . . The film has the lightness of a bird coasting." *Newsweek* was even more ebullient, describing the film as "so brilliant" that it ranks "with the best ever made in Latin America. . . . [It] is clearly a masterpiece—a film that is intricate, ironic, and extremely intelligent."*

This study of the degeneration of a middle-class intellectual paralyzed by the revolution is almost clinical in its accuracy. Sergio, the protagonist, is apolitical, neither revolutionary nor counterrevolutionary. He favors the Revolution because of his vengeance against the bourgeoisie and its values, including his own. A former furniture dealer, he is now without useful occupation, living off the revolution's confiscation payments. His wife

---

* The film is now available for rentals to educational groups from the newly formed Center for Cuban Studies, 186 West Fourth Street, New York, N.Y. 10014. The Center will soon have other Cuban films on hand.

has "crossed the bridge" to the United States. He sits and stares, without will, without purpose. The great movement around him has rendered him defunct, fossilized. Interspersed with Sergio's saga are pieces of news footage—the counterrevolutionary bombing of a Havana department store, the defeat of CIA mercenaries at Playa Girón, preparation for the showdown with John F. Kennedy during the "Crisis of October." The events dominate Sergio as he is incapable of participation in them.

Edmundo Desnoes describes the film in an issue of the Cuban film magazine *Cine Cubano*:

A shapeless idea which I had in my mind and which had remained abstract in the book, has been objectified. The subjective elements of a diary have been given a social density. I have shown the antecedents of the character with documentaries of the world torn by revolution. Sergio is the product, although he might deny it, of the same world which produced Batista and the ridiculous parties of an ignorant and vulgar upper middle class. That world thought it could return when the incident of Playa Girón occurred. I could almost say that Titon [Alea] has understood better than I have the essential conflict of the novel: the struggle between the best products of the bourgeois way of life—education, travel and money—and an authentic revolution. Sergio's criticism is never revolutionary, it is only an escape valve to strengthen the established order; but that order is dead. That is the tragedy of Sergio; his irony, his intelligence, is a defensive mechanism which prevents him from becoming involved in the reality. Titon manages to explain this with pictures, in concrete cinematographic situations. The key of the character is that he does not assume his historical involvement: he cannot accept underdevelopment but is incapable of facing the necessary risks to overcome it. The character's world is closed; the revolution, however, is open to everybody. . . .

This remoteness—subjectiveness, photographs, documentary films—allows us to see what is our own as something strange. Art today in the Revolution is also exorcism to untangle the present from the past. Sergio is alive on the screen but yet, at the same time, he died in the Revolution. The republic is something of yesterday, Batista is a beast from another world: everything seems to be as unreal as a nightmare and as remote as the nostalgic memories of the old. That death which Gutiérrez Alea puts across to us, that world which no longer exists (we shall never return to the brothels, we shall never again study in schools run by priests, we shall never find ourselves again in the great parties of the bourgeoisie, in the workshops of *La Marina*,* nor shall we see students thrashed in San Lazaro street) that world on the screen makes us feel and think. It is perturbing and ambiguous. Even the present appears at a distance: Sergio comes in between the two.

Sergio is an outsider to the Revolution. And, Alea says, a state which wishes to stay alive cannot afford a predominance of outsiders. The film concludes with scenes of feverish preparation for the missile crisis of 1962. Kennedy has dared Cuba, and Fidel, audacious and proud as ever, replies: "We know what we are doing and we know how to defend our independence. They threaten us by saying we'll be nuclear targets. It doesn't scare us. We have to know how to live during the age we happen to live in, with the dignity to know how to live, every man and woman, young and old, we are all one in this hour of danger,

* A right-wing newspaper during Batista's time.

and it is the same for all of us, revolutionaries and patriots, and victory shall be for all." For all, except Sergio, who remains aloof, staring through binoculars from the verandah of his expensive apartment at his compatriots as they prepare again to do battle.

According to the ICAIC the film had no shooting script. What follows is a script composed, by this book's editor, of the English version's subtitles and the setting and changing of scenes, recorded during several screenings of the film.

Credits

Script:	Tomás Gutiérrez Alea and Edmundo Desnoes, based on the novel by Edmundo Desnoes
Director of photography:	Ramón F. Suárez
Production director:	Tomás Gutiérrez Alea
Editor:	Nelson Rodríguez
Music:	Leo Brower
Conducted by:	Manuel Duchezne Cuzán
With a special performance by:	Pello el Afrocán
Assistant directors:	Ingeborg Hot Seeland Jesús Hernández
First assistant cameraman:	Alberto Menéndez
Assistant to the producer:	Jesús Pascaux
Script girl:	Babi Díaz
Produced by:	Miguel Mendoza
Sound engineers:	Eugenio Vesa Germinal Hernández Carlos Fernández
Musical recording:	Medardo Montero EGREM Studios
Set designer:	Julio Matilla
Make-up:	María Consuelo Ventura Isabel Amezaga

Properties:	Orlando González
Wardrobe:	Elba Perez
Lighting:	Enrique González
Grip:	Juan García
Head of construction:	Luis Obregon
Stills:	José Luis Rodríguez
Photographs by:	Luz Chessex
Titles:	Umberto Pena
Animation:	Roberto Riquenes
Optical effects:	Jorge Pucheux

The film was produced on black-and-white 35-mm. film and runs 104 minutes

Prizes: Mermaid, Warsaw Festival, 1970
Three special prizes, Hyères, France, 1970
London Film Festival, 1971

Cast:

Sergio Corrieri (*Sergio*)
Daisy Granados (*Elena*)
Eslinda Núñez (*Noemí*)
Omar Valdés
René de la Cruz

Yolanda Farr
Ofelia Gonzáles
José Gil Abad
Daniel Jordan
Luis López
Rafael Sosa

MEMORIES OF
UNDERDEVELOPMENT

(Opening shot: Carnival scene, bongos playing while crowd is dancing chaotically. Shots are heard in the background, almost unnoticed, as a man is lifted on shoulders and carried out through the milling crowd. Over this scene flash the titles and credits.)

(Cut to José Martí International Airport. Families crying, waving.)

(SCREEN TITLE): HAVANA, 1961. MANY PEOPLE ARE LEAVING THE COUNTRY.

(Cut to Passport Control. Sergio's wife and parents are departing. He embraces them, but it is obvious he feels nothing and is awkward in the situation. He cannot properly say goodbye. The exit papers are finally signed. His wife turns tearfully away and departs for the plane while Sergio is heard, voice over.)

SERGIO *(voice over)*: She'll have to go to work there . . . Well, that is, until she finds some dumb guy who'll marry her. To tell the truth, she's still something to look at . . .

(Cut to Sergio on the bus ride back to town, musing as camera cuts back and forth from bus to airport farewell scene.)

SERGIO *(voice over)*: She'll remember me as long as she's having a rough time, after that . . . I'm the one who's really been stupid. Working so that she could live like someone who had been born in New York or Paris, and not in this underdeveloped island . . .

MILITIAMAN *(getting off the bus)*: Excuse me.

(Cut to Sergio's apartment. He is restless and wanders from room to room. Camera closes in on birds chirping on apartment balcony's edge.

Cut back to Sergio in bedroom, removing tie and shoes. He collapses on bed.

Cut to Sergio at his typewriter.

Cut to paper in typewriter as keys write.)

(TYPEWRITER): All those who loved and nagged me up to the last moment have already gone . . .

(Cut to the kitchen. Sergio, now in underwear, makes coffee and toast. He relaxes, sips coffee, and belches.)

SERGIO *(voice over)*:   I've been saying for years that if I had the time I would sit down and write a book of stories or a diary; now I'll find out if I have anything to say . . .

(Cut to Sergio going out to balcony. Through his binoculars we follow him focusing on lovers on an adjacent hotel roof; to long shot of ships in Havana Harbor; to defense preparations; to dismantled statue in honor of the U.S. Maine; to billboard on nearby building with a political slogan; meanwhile he talks, voice over.)

SERGIO *(voice over)*:
(Lovers on roof):
Everything is the same. Here everything is the same. All of a sudden it looks like a set, a city of cardboard.

(Ship in harbor):
The Bronze Titan . . .

(Defense preparations):
Cuba, free and independent . . . Who would have thought that this could happen?

(Dismantled Maine *statue)*:
Without the imperial eagle.
Where is the dove Picasso was going to send?
It's very comfortable being a communist millionaire in Paris.

(Billboard):
"This great humanity has said enough and has started to move forward."*

* The quote, seen throughout Cuba, is from the Second Declaration of Havana, read by Fidel in 1962, spelling out the goals of the Cuban Revolution.

Like my parents, like Laura, and they won't stop until they get
to Miami.
However, today everything looks so different.
Have I changed or has the city changed?
It is the time of departure . . .
Oh! abandoned like the wharves at dawn.
Everything in you was like a shipwreck.

*(Cut to Sergio removing dead bird from cage. Drops it off bal-
cony and yawns.*

*Cut to tape recorder. Sergio pushes the start button and listens.
While he rummages through Laura's closet he tries on her furs,
opens her drawer, and caresses in order her left-behind powder
puffs, pearls, eyeglasses, lipstick. We see him playing with the
lipstick, twisting it up and down. He takes the stick and doodles
on her mirror. He rummages through her underwear.*

Cut to flashback of Laura stepping into shower.

Cut to Sergio taking her stocking, pulling it over his head, and gazing in the mirror at his horribly distorted image. All of this while we hear over the tape recorder.)

SERGIO: What are you doing?

LAURA: Can't you see?

SERGIO: I mean, what are you reading?

LAURA: Something banal, frivolous, and superficial. *The Best of Everything.*

SERGIO: Oh, yes. That film . . .

LAURA: Yes. Leave me alone, please.

SERGIO: Me?

LAURA: Yes. You're looking at me as if I were some strange insect. I can't read like this.

SERGIO: Why don't we talk a little?

LAURA: What's bitten you?

SERGIO: You can only talk about insects lately.

LAURA: What am I going to talk about when we're surrounded by insects all day? This country is falling behind, as you say.

SERGIO: What do you think?

LAURA: Why do you say that? You've never been interested in what I think about anything . . .

SERGIO: You're practicing your English a lot lately. I think you intend to leave.

LAURA: Leave me alone!

SERGIO: I like you more when you get vulgar . . . That always excites me, when I see you struggle between elegance and vulgarity.

LAURA: I've been looking at you for some time now and you're looking really strange. Lately you're rather disgusting.

SERGIO: It's that I don't have any Yardley's hair lotion, or any Colgate toothpaste, or any after-shave lotion . . . As you know, all that helps a lot.

LAURA: Yes, it must be that . . .

SERGIO: And yet you get more attractive each day. You're more artificial. I don't like natural beauty. I like women like you, who are made with good clothes, good food, make-up, massages. Thanks to that you have stopped being a slovenly Cuban girl.

LAURA: I never know when you're telling the truth or when you're kidding.

SERGIO: A little of both, darling.

LAURA: Well, go kid your mother, darling.

SERGIO: Ha, ha, ha!

LAURA: Go to hell!

SERGIO: That's very good!

LAURA: Are you crazy, stupid? Let me go. I can't stand you, I can't stand living here any longer, I can't stand the heat. You stink. Let me go.

SERGIO: Everything you said was taped.

LAURA: What?

SERGIO: Everything. Word for word. It'll be fun later on, when you hear it.

LAURA: You monster! You're sick! I'm going to smash the tape recorder!

SERGIO: Be careful, you'll break it!

(Cut to Sergio turning off tape recorder, slowly removing Laura's stocking from his head, and falling into bed.

Cut to downtown Havana. The streets are busy as people move briskly along. The camera follows girls in school uniforms and women in curlers. The camera's eye is also Sergio's, as we follow the women strolling. Then into a bookstore: the racks

show a mixture of Engels and Lenin together with cheap novels.
Sergio continues to eye the women.)

SERGIO *(voice over)*:   Here women look into your eyes as if
they would like to be touched by your look. That only happens
here.
People only look after their own problems.
Maybe Italian women gaze a little longer, but no, it's never like
here.

(Cut to newsreel of Havana department store on fire.)

SERGIO *(voice over)*:   Since El Encanto* burned down, Havana
is like a country town. To think they once called her the Paris
of the Caribbean.

(Cut to Sergio again walking the street, staring at store windows,
all empty except for the occasional poster of Martí or Fidel.)

SERGIO *(voice over)*:   That's what the tourists and the whores
used to call her.
Now it looks more like a Tegucigalpa of the Caribbean.
It's not only because there are few good things in the stores.
It's also because of the people.

(Cut to various faces in the crowd, old and young, all serious
or worried.)

SERGIO *(voice over)*:   What meaning has life for them? What
meaning has it for me? But I'm not like them!

(SCREEN TITLE):   PABLO.

(Cut to Pablo and Sergio talking as they drive along the Malecon,
Havana's sea-front drive. As they talk, the camera cuts from

---

* Havana's main department store was destroyed by bombs set off by
  counterrevolutionaries in 1960.

*them to a night club with the two of them and their wives; to a
hotel pool as the two of them watch the women.)*

PABLO: These people say they're making the first socialist
revolution in America. So what? They're going back to the
jungle . . . they'll go hungry . . . Like the Haitians . . . They
beat Napoleon and . . . so? They had the most important sugar
industry in the world before the revolution, and look at them
now.

SERGIO: Times change.

PABLO: Besides, this is a problem between Russians and
Americans; we have nothing to do with it. Listen to me, Sergio,
this whole thing is going to blow up . . . We're going to catch the
first punch either of them throws, and you know why? Because
we're so small, a teeny tiny island. It will be you who'll catch
the punch, because I won't be here.

SERGIO *(voice over):* To think that we've been friends for more
than five years.

PABLO: Under Batista things had reached the point where you
couldn't take it any longer. Not for me, I never got involved
with politics. I have a clear conscience. The only thing I've done
all my life is to work. To work like an animal. Can you imagine
Anita? So beautiful and yet her stomach is stuffed with black
beans. They definitely have all the means to develop this
country's economy. Fully . . .

(Cut to gas station, as Pablo pulls in for refueling.)

SERGIO: The "know-how"?

PABLO: Yes, the "know-how." The Americans know how to
do things, they know how to make things run.

GARAGE EMPLOYEE: Three.

PABLO: Check the oil.

GARAGE EMPLOYEE: Haven't got any . . . If you want I can check it anyway.

PABLO: No. What for? I've got to hand it in in the same condition as it was before.

SERGIO: Why?

(Cut to car veering back onto Malecon. They drive a bit further. Cut to a different garage this time. Sergio looking through windshield at Pablo and Garage Mechanic negotiating.)

PABLO: It's been inventoried. If I don't hand it in like it was, I can't leave . . .

MECHANIC: I can't get the sealed unit. You'll have to do that yourself. Things aren't what they used to be . . .

PABLO: Yes, I know that.

MECHANIC: It will not look the same. If you can't get wood alcohol, you'll have to use synthetic paint, which isn't the same. You'll have to paint at least this part so it won't look bad.

PABLO: What about this dent?

(As Sergio continues to stare, cut to a series of still photos of various Latin American countries gripped by poverty—infants with protruding stomachs, people sheltered in caves, etc.)

SERGIO *(voice over)*:   He says the only thing a Cuban can't stand is hunger. All the starvation we've gone through since the Spaniards came! In Latin America four children die every minute due to illnesses . . . caused by malnutrition. After ten years there will be 20 million children dead. The same number of deaths caused by the Second World War.

(Cut to Pablo's car parked at home. Pablo and Sergio get out and approach another car. Pablo steals a headlight.)

PABLO: It's a symbol of decadence. But I feel better. That way I don't have to go on fixing it.

SERGIO: Well, if you like to walk.

PABLO: No, but I feel more at ease. I don't have any problems. They say the latest American cars are incredible. I was reading a magazine Julio had lent me. Sealed motors with two spark plugs and a two-year guarantee. If it breaks down they give you another one. With the mechanics we have here, that's the solution.

SERGIO *(voice over)*: People seem to me more stupid.

(Cut for a second to same night club scene with Pablo and his wife, Sergio and Laura.)

LAURA: Pablo is right. All the French stink.

PABLO: They're just naturally dirty . . .

(Cut to Pablo's apartment. Pablo is washing his hands and face while Sergio watches.)

PABLO: It's the same to me if they take it all. I don't care! But now I'm not going to stay at home and do nothing like when they were fighting Batista. The truth is I never thought they could overthrow him. I must do something now or I won't be able to operate when this thing blows up.

SERGIO: That's what they said.

PABLO: Who?

SERGIO: The Bay of Pigs prisoners.

PABLO: Oh! Listen to me.

(Cut to newsreel of the CIA invasion at Playa Girón; captured mercenaries with their hands over their heads; close-up stills of various types of prisoners.)

(SCREEN TITLE): THE TRUTH OF THE GROUP IS IN THE MURDERER

SERGIO *(voice over)*: We found under the military organization of the invaders an order in the social duties that summarizes the division in the moral and social functions of the bourgeoisie:
the priest
the free-enterprise man
the dilettante official
the torturer
the philosopher
the politician
and the innumerable sons of good families.
Each one of them carried out specific duties, and yet it was the whole, the group, which gave meaning to each individual activity. Calvino was a murderer who caused horror and scorn even among the burgeoisie.

(Cut to newsreel of women milicianas *giving testimony before military tribunal.)*

WITNESS 1: The housecoat I wore . . . There are still bloodstains in front . . . Because he kicked me in the stomach and I had a hemorrhage. That wasn't enough for him. I had to fight so they wouldn't do that, and they broke two of my vertebrae . . . Do you remember?

WITNESS 2: . . . When they started hitting him with sticks, you also hit him. He fell on his knees and you kicked him in the side and he fell on the floor. Do you remember?

JOURNALIST: So after you murdered him you abused him also?

WITNESS 2:   He's a murderer!

WITNESS 3:   You shot him and then laughed at the way he died!

CALVINO *(mercenary)*:   Excuse me . . .

WITNESS 2:   October 6th, at seven o'clock in the evening.

CALVINO: Listen to me.

WITNESS 3:   . . . and say it isn't so. Say it isn't true that after you killed Morua, nine days later you told me how you had killed him. Say it, Calvino.

CALVINO: I can't answer her.

(Cut to newsreel shots of the dictator Batista looking over various firearms; to stills of Batista and of atrocities committed against rebels in the attack on the Moncada Barracks;* newsreels of prerevolutionry society balls and street riots.)

SERGIO *(voice over)*:   In all capitalist societies there is this same type of man at the disposal of the bourgeoisie, who is in charge of such singular duties. In the division of moral work the murderer permits the existence of those who are not directly in contact with death, and as separate individuals want to keep their souls clean.

MERCENARY 1:   I'm talking for myself and for those who think like me. We might be in the minority. I'm not talking for Ventura nor for those miserable creatures that have been named. I didn't even know Calvino at that time. I was just interested in living my own life.

---

* This attack, on July 26, 1953, on the Batista army barracks in Santiago de Cuba, was led by Fidel Castro and signaled the beginning of the armed struggle against the dictator.

SERGIO *(voice over)*:   They appear like disjointed elements of a totality which nobody assumes completely.

MERCENARY 1:   I can't answer for the others. Because everybody answers for himself.

MERCENARY 2:   It seems like you want to accuse me of being the originator of the invasion. I want to insist that my mission was purely spiritual. I have never handled a weapon. The fact that one is mixed up in the conspiracy doesn't make him a conspirator.

MERCENARY 3:   I've told you that I have never been a political person. I never had anything to do with any political party, and also, it's your personal behavior that frees you from responsibility.

(Cut to more stills in close-up of each Mercenary; more stills of atrocities; newsreel cutting from ceremonial affairs with the old bourgeois political rulers, to broken bodies lying along country roads.)

SERGIO *(voice over)*:   Everybody refers to his own personality when he wants to get away from another person's contaminating misery. . . . Or he sinks into the group when he has to hide his own responsibility.

MERCENARY 4:   We are now a group. I'm not the only one now.

SERGIO *(voice over)*:   It can be seen how that responsibility, repelled by all, is returned and recovered by a member of the same group.

MERCENARY 4:   No; you're talking of the group's cause; it isn't mine.

SERGIO *(voice over)*:   In fact, the murderer-torturer resorts to the category of totality in order to claim his moral irresponsibility.

MERCENARY 4:   Listen, I've committed no direct crime, I'm telling you.

SERGIO *(voice over)*:   But in none of the cases considered was there a recovery of the true dialectic relationship between individuals and the group. The others who came with Calvino don't recognize themselves as part of the system which entangles them in their own acts.
In the accounts of Freyre, the land baron;
in the extreme unction of Lugo, the priest;
in the reasonings of Andreu, the philosopher;
in the dismissals and in the book of Rivero,
the dilettante; in the "representative
democracy" of Varone, who could read clearly
the death which through them spread over Cuba,
death by hunger, by sickness,
by torture, by frustration?

(SCREEN TITLE):   NOEMÍ.

(Cut to Sergio's kitchen. Noemí is making coffee. They sit and chat. When she speaks, the camera is on him.)

SERGIO *(voice over)*:   She comes three times a week to clean the apartment. She's been coming for over a year and I've never noticed her.
If she would fix herself up and dress better she would be very attractive.
She's as thin as a *Vogue* model.
I like her.
Born in Matanzas and a Protestant. A Baptist, I think.

SERGIO: Did they baptize you in a river?

NOEMÍ: Of course . . .

SERGIO: And then . . .

NOEMÍ: Well.

SERGIO: Can't I know?

(Cut to Sergio's imaginary "resurrection," as he and she make love standing up in a shallow river, the mist surrounding them, Vivaldi playing in the background. Meanwhile, Noemí is in fact recalling her baptism.)

NOEMÍ: The group gathered at the edge of the river; the pastor and I went into the water. Afterwards he told me what baptism means. It symbolizes the death of sin, the resurrection of a new life full of faith, of hope, of dignity. Then he took me to the deepest part and put me under. If you could have seen how scared I was! But everything happened so quickly I didn't even notice. All that anxiety and all that fuss, for nothing.

(Cut to Sergio sitting over his typewriter, not typing. He watches Noemí clean house, as he daydreams of them in bed.)

SERGIO *(voice over)*: Almost everybody is an exhibitionist. They generally give me the impression of defenselessness, almost hairless animals, balanced precariously on two legs. Someone once said man's intelligence and physical imperfection are due to the fact that he is the premature fetus of the monkey.

(Cut to Sergio in swimming trunks and U.S. college sweatshirt, strolling along the edge of a hotel swimming pool. As usual, he is watching the women.)

SERGIO *(voice over)*: There is an exquisite moment between thirty and thirty-five when Cuban women suddenly pass from maturity to poverty.
They are fruits which rot at an amazing speed.

(Cut to television screen. Though reception is bad, we see Marilyn Monroe singing in an old movie. The channel changes to a newsreel. We see U.S. soldiers throwing rocks and making obscene gestures at the camera.)

TV NARRATOR: And the rule of the Yankee empire having been ended by the revolution, the United States now uses the Guantánamo Naval Base as an espionage center in Cuba. ICAIC cameramen film some of the provocations of military personnel and counterrevolutionaries exiled on the base.

(SCREEN TITLE):   ELENA.

(Cut to La Rampa, Havana's main nightlife strip. It is daytime. Sergio, walking along in a suit and tie, spots Elena. The camera follows him as he stares at her, then follows her as she walks away, flirtatiously. Sergio approaches Elena. The camera zooms in on Elena as she strolls along, making herself a little available. As Sergio catches up to her, a midget carrying a cello walks by. This makes Elena smile, breaking the ice.)

SERGIO: You have beautiful knees! Do you want to have dinner with me?

ELENA: Are you crazy?

SERGIO: No. I just don't like to eat alone. What are you doing here? Waiting for someone? Your boy friend?

ELENA: Are you crazy?

SERGIO: At your age it's dangerous to be alone around here.

ELENA: You are crazy!

SERGIO: No, look, really. Why don't you come with me? I can't digest properly when I eat alone.

(Cut to a restaurant waiter taking their orders. Then to the two of them over dinner.)

ELENA: I'm waiting for someone from ICAIC who called me about a job.

SERGIO: From ICAIC?

ELENA: They're going to test me for a film.

SERGIO: I have a friend who's pretty important there. He's a director, I believe.

ELENA: At ICAIC?

SERGIO: Yes. If you want, I'll introduce him to you.

ELENA: What time is it?

SERGIO: Around six-thirty.

ELENA: He's late. He won't come now.

SERGIO: Are you coming . . . ?
Bring me a dry martini first . . . Why don't you have something to drink?

ELENA: I can't drink. I'm taking these shots for my nerves. Look . . .

SERGIO: Why do you want to be an actress?

ELENA: Because I'm tired of always being the same. That way I can be someone else without people thinking I'm crazy. I want to unfold my personality.

(Cut to old Hollywood movie scenes, each being repeated over and over again. First, a couple making love on the beach; the man crawls onto the woman, then again, then again and again. Next, a woman stepping into the shower, repeated several times. A stripper taking off her bra and panties repeatedly. Sergio is heard voice over.)

SERGIO *(voice over)*:   But all those characters are like scratched records. The only thing an actress does is to repeat the same movements and the same words thousands of times. The same movements and the same words.

(Cut to the film stopping, lights snapped on. Then cut to an

ICAIC screening room, the next day. Elena is dressed differently.)

SERGIO: Where did you get them?

TOMÁS GUTIÉRREZ ALEA: They showed up one day. These are the cuts the Commission made.

PROJECTIONIST: The Revisory Commission. What we used to have before the Revolution. Those are the shots they took out.

TOMÁS GUTIÉRREZ ALEA: They said they were offensive to morals and good breeding.

SERGIO: It looks like they also had their moral preoccupations. At least they worried about keeping up a front. What are you going to do with them?

TOMÁS GUTIÉRREZ ALEA: I'm thinking of using them.

SERGIO: In a film?

TOMÁS GUTIÉRREZ ALEA: Yes.

SERGIO: It will have to have a meaning.

(Cut to Sergio, Elena, and Alea exiting screening room. The camera withdraws ahead of them as they walk down the hall.)

TOMÁS GUTIÉRREZ ALEA: It's coming along. You'll see.

SERGIO: Will they release it?

TOMÁS GUTIÉRREZ ALEA: Yes. It'll be a collage that'll have a bit of everything.

SERGIO: Let's see Daisy.

(Cut to Elena against the wall of an office, being interviewed.)

INTERVIEWER: What's your experience? Have you worked in the theatre, TV, or something?

ELENA: No. I haven't had any luck.

INTERVIEWER: Have you studied?

ELENA: I was going to take some classes once, but . . . I didn't.

INTERVIEWER: Well, write that in on the form.

ELENA: Aren't you going to try me out now? I can also sing.

(Cut to Elena auditioning terribly as the camera pans the on-looking faces, astonished.)

ELENA: This sadness rejects oblivion
Like darkness rejects light;
I hope destiny lets you return
One day, to remember . . .

(Cut to Elena and Sergio strolling on a neighborhood street, flirting with each other.)

SERGIO: If you say so . . . And you?

ELENA: No.

SERGIO: Sure that it's no?

ELENA: Sure.

(Cut to Elena and Sergio stopping at the gates of a mansion.)

SERGIO: What a beautiful house! Like it?

ELENA: I don't know.

(Cut to Elena running from Sergio. He catches her and they join hands.)

ELENA: You don't think that we'll do anything.

(Cut to the front of Sergio's apartment building.)

SERGIO: Look, there's where I live. Come on. What's the matter?

ELENA: I don't . . .

SERGIO: Don't what?

ELENA: And your wife?

SERGIO: Didn't I tell you I'm divorced?

ELENA: Well, even then . . .

SERGIO: Even then what?

ELENA: What'll the neighbors think?

SERGIO: Well, if you don't trust me . . .

ELENA: It isn't that.

SERGIO: What is it then?

ELENA: Well. You go up first.

SERGIO: On the top floor, apartment K-L.

(Cut to Sergio entering his apartment hurriedly. He frantically rearranges the apartment, hiding girlie magazines and used drinking glasses. He neatens his hair, turns the radio on to a

music station, and prepares the liquor cabinet. He answers the doorbell. Elena enters, hesitatingly, shyly.)

SERGIO: Make yourself comfortable. I'll make some coffee.

(Cut to Elena staring silently at the room and all of its objets d'art. Cut to Elena on the sofa, more comfortable than before. She jauntily gets up and changes the radio station to pop music. Her eye catches an old photograph. Sergio enters, carrying drinks. He sits down on the couch but she remains standing.)

SERGIO: They're my parents. That's Laura. They left the same day.

ELENA: And you?

SERGIO: I, what?

ELENA: Aren't you leaving?

SERGIO: I'm fine right here.

(Cut to Elena joining Sergio on the couch.)

ELENA: Are you a revolutionary?

SERGIO: What do you think?

ELENA: That you're neither a revolutionary nor a counter-revolutionary.

(Cut to Sergio making a pass at Elena, but she eludes him.)

SERGIO: Then what am I?

ELENA: You're nothing.
They'll send you things.

SERGIO: What for?

ELENA: Nice shoes. What do I know? They could even send you a car.

SERGIO: Laura had a figure like yours more or less. If you want, I can show you some of her dresses. If you like them you can keep them.

ELENA: But . . .

SERGIO: Look at them anyway.

(Cut to Sergio staring out of window.

Cut back to Elena coming out of the bedroom in a new dress.)

SERGIO: You look fine. Take a look.

ELENA: You'll have to button me up.

(The camera cuts to a full-length mirror as we see Sergio button-ing the dress from behind Elena. They embrace and kiss. She breaks away and begins to cry. Sergio approaches her, and again they embrace and kiss. And again she breaks away.

Cut to the bedroom. Elena is half-undressed, sticking her tongue out, teasing Sergio. He catches her and they kiss again, as she alternately lures and repulses him. Finally he corners her on the bed, and they make love.

Cut to Elena crying in the background. It is an hour later. Sergio moves to comfort Elena.)

ELENA: No . . .
No, no, no . . .

SERGIO: Come on, don't cry.
Please don't . . .

ELENA: You've ruined me!

SERGIO: Who, me?
We haven't done anything wrong . . .

ELENA: What am I going to tell my mother?

SERGIO: Don't tell her anything.

(Cut to Sergio putting Laura's old clothes in a shopping bag for Elena. She pretends to refuse his offer.)

SERGIO: If you wait a minute, I'll go with you.

ELENA: No. I want to be alone.

SERGIO: Call me.

(Cut to Sergio's doorway. Elena leaves as he stares after her. Camera now follows Sergio around the apartment as he remembers—Laura's dresser, Laura's closet.

Cut to previous "tape recorder" scene with Laura.)

SERGIO: . . . Thanks to that you have stopped being a slovenly Cuban girl.

LAURA: I never know when you're telling the truth or when you're kidding.

SERGIO: A little of both, darling.

LAURA: Well, go kid your mother, darling.
Go to hell!

SERGIO: That's very good!

LAURA: Are you crazy, stupid? Let me go. I can't stand you, I can't stand living here any longer, I can't stand the heat. You stink. Let me go.

SERGIO: Everything you said was taped.

LAURA: What?

SERGIO: Everything. Word for word. It'll be fun later on, when you hear it.

LAURA: You monster! You're sick! I'm going to smash the tape recorder!

SERGIO: Be careful, you'll break it!

LAURA: I don't care!

SERGIO: Let go, you'll . . .

LAURA: Give it to me!
Let me go! We're through! I never want to see you again!
I'm leaving. I'm going alone. I don't want you to come with me.

SERGIO: So, you want to leave me?

LAURA: I don't care!

SERGIO: Didn't you used to say . . .

LAURA: I won't be a guinea pig for your whims and little games. I'm going to live my own life! I'm getting old! Do you hear! Old! I'm going alone! I'm leaving! I don't want to be with you! I'm leaving!

(Cut to Sergio in his bathroom, the next morning, brushing teeth. The doorbell rings. Sergio puts on his pants to answer the door. It is Elena. She enters, singing, kissing him, cheerful and confident. Now she is at home.)

SERGIO: What's this . . . ?

ELENA: Before your lips confirmed
that you loved me,
I already knew it,
I already knew it.

SERGIO: Are you all right now?

ELENA: Who, me?

SERGIO: I thought you didn't feel well.

ELENA: I didn't, but I'm all right now. I came to see how you were. If you like, I can help you make lunch.
What's wrong with you?

SERGIO: Nothing at all . . .

ELENA: Go on and say it,
It couldn't last,
It's all finished,
It couldn't be,
You don't love me any more . . .
Do you like the song?

(Cut to Elena planting herself in the middle of the room. Sergio approaches her. Again she moves away, teasingly.)

SERGIO: Then all that crying last night?

ELENA: Don't make fun of me.

SERGIO: I'm not making fun of you.

ELENA: You just don't have any feelings . . .
You don't have to criticize the way I live.
If all I have now . . .

(Cut to a series of contrasting stills of Elena, playing for the camera.)

SERGIO *(voice over)*: One of the things that really gets me about people is their inability to sustain a feeling, an idea, without falling apart. Elena proved to be totally inconsistent. It's pure alteration, as Ortega would say. She doesn't relate things.

(Cut to Havana street scenes, filled with women.)

SERGIO *(voice over)*: That's one of the signs of underdevelopment: the inability to relate things, to accumulate experience and to develop . . . It is difficult because here one produces a woman shaped by sentiments and culture.

(Cut to Sergio driving Pablo to the airport. They pass a billboard: Fidel and Playa Girón.

Cut to airport ticket desk, as Pablo and Sergio approach. Pablo is on crutches.)

SERGIO *(voice over)*: It's a soft environment.
Cubans waste their talents adapting themselves to every moment.
People aren't consistent.
And they always need someone to think for them.

PABLO: I hope I see you soon, Sergio.

SERGIO: I don't think so. I already know the States and what's going to happen here is a mystery to me.

PABLO: Everybody knows what's going to happen here.

SERGIO: Well, I don't. I really don't.

PABLO: It won't be like the Bay of Pigs.

SERGIO: Maybe, but that could have interesting results.

PABLO: That's true. But I want to be on the other side.

SERGIO: You'll be safer. And you'll also be able to see old friends.

PABLO: I know what you're driving at.

SERGIO: Yes?

PABLO: Yes. But there are also decent people amongst them.

SERGIO: At least that's what they say.

PABLO: I don't know if they say that or not. I've got a clean conscience.

SERGIO: You, yes.

(Cut to Pablo on the other side of a glass partition separating him from Sergio and the camera in the airport reception room. Pablo gestures broadly to Sergio, but the latter is filled with his own thoughts.)

SERGIO *(voice over)*:   Was I like him, before?
It's possible.
Although it may destroy me, this Revolution is my revenge against the stupid Cuban bourgeoisie.
Against idiots like Pablo.
I realize that Pablo isn't Pablo; it's my own life.

Everything I don't want to be.
It's good to see them leave.
Just as if I threw them up.
I keep my mind clear.
It's a disagreeable clarity, empty.
I know what's happening to me but I can't avoid it.
He, Laura, everybody . . .

(Cut to Sergio walking along Havana side streets. He recalls his childhood—a mansion that housed a boyhood friend . . .)

SERGIO *(voice over)*:   Francisco de la Cuesta lived here.
We were eight or ten years old.
Where is Francisco now?
Does he remember our games?
I try to and I can't.

(Cut to a military school. The children are in olive green uniforms.

Cut to same school with a priest and children, this time in Catholic school uniforms.)

SERGIO *(voice over)*:   When we were at school, the priests were always right.
They had the power then.
I hadn't done anything, but it was all the same.
I understood then, for the first time, the relationship between Justice and Power.

(Cut to a Havana slum neighborhood at night. Sergio, now a shy teen-ager, approaches a whorehouse with his friend. The house is cheap, smelly, and slovenly. The teen-age Sergio un-

dresses. He is ignorant, but the prostitute instructs him how to proceed.)

SERGIO *(voice over)*:   Armando's father was a freethinker.
Every week he'd give him a peso so he could go to a whorehouse.
He took me for the first time.
To a fat woman who charged fifty cents.
He told her to be nice to me.
But I couldn't do anything with her.
I had to find another.
After that I went every week.

(Cut to Sergio today, back in the bookstore. He browses through the shelves while Elena stands near the door, biting her nails, waiting for him.)

SERGIO *(voice over)*:   All of a sudden I discovered that Elena didn't think the way I did.
I had expected more of her.
I thought she was more complex and interesting.

(Cut to Havana's Bellas Artes Museum. Sergio tries to point out things for Elena to look for. As they go from gallery to gallery, Elena trails behind Sergio.)

SERGIO *(voice over)*:   I always try to live like a European.
And Elena forces me to feel underdeveloped at every step.
I also tried to change Elena.

(Cut to Sergio, still in the Museum, staring at a painting. Elena approaches and straightens his tie. This art is beyond her.)

SERGIO *(voice over)*:   And like Laura . . .
She doesn't understand.

She has another world in her head, very different from mine. She doesn't see me.

(SCREEN TITLE): A TROPICAL ADVENTURE.

(Cut to the Ernest Hemingway house, now the Hemingway Museum. The Guide prattles on . . .)

GUIDE: This gazelle was shot by Hemingway during his last trip to Africa in 1953. He made that trip with Mary, his fourth wife. This is one of the fastest gazelles in Africa. Besides being very fast it's constantly jumping . . .

(Cut back to Sergio, who breaks away, deep in his own thoughts.)

SERGIO *(voice over)*: He said he killed so as not to kill himself. But in the end he couldn't resist the temptation.

(Cut to Robert Capa's still photos of the Spanish Civil War.)

GUIDE: We know Hemingway made several trips to Spain as a war correspondent. And after that he joined the International Brigade . . .

(Cut back to the Hemingway house. Elena and Sergio are in one room, alone together.)

ELENA: Is this where Mr. Way used to live? I don't see anything so special. Books and dead animals. Just like the American house in Preston. The same furniture and the same American smell.

SERGIO: What is an American smell?

ELENA: I don't know. You feel it.

SERGIO: Which do you like best, the smell of the Russians or of the Americans?

ELENA: Leave me alone. I don't know anything about politics.

(Cut to Sergio looking over Hemingway's rifles, dead game mounted on the walls. The Guide continues to lecture, and Elena listens intently but quickly becomes bored. She poses for photographs for some foreign tourist.)

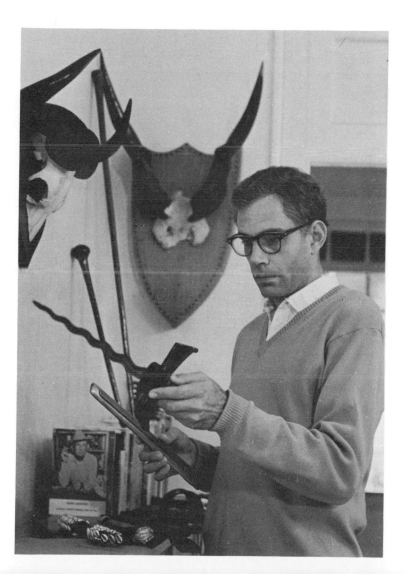

SERGIO *(voice over)*: The tropics. That's what backward countries are for: to kill animals, to fish, and to sunbathe . . . There you have her: the beautiful Cuban señorita . . .

(Cut to Sergio, leafing through one of the books from Hemingway's collection.)

SERGIO *(voice over)*:   "I don't think I'd ever be afraid of anything again," Macomber said to Wilson. "Something happened inside me when we saw the buffalo for the first time. Like a dam bursting. It was pure excitement."
As if running after a buffalo was enough to conquer fear. Anyway, there are no buffalo in Cuba.
I'm an idiot.
He conquered the fear of death but he couldn't stand the fear of life, of time, of a world that was beginning to get too large.

(Cut to the House. Elena returns briefly.)

ELENA: Why did you leave?

SERGIO: You were amusing yourself.

ELENA: Jealousy.

SERGIO: Oh, please!

ELENA: Does it bother you?

SERGIO: No, it doesn't.

ELENA: You don't care.

SERGIO: About what?

ELENA: Me.

SERGIO: You're the one who doesn't care. You don't care about anything.

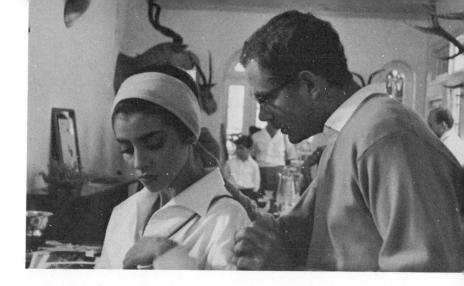

(Cut to the Guide and his group entering the room.)

GUIDE: This is Hemingway's private study. He could always be found working in front of this old typewriter. He never sat down to write, nor did he wear shoes. He'd get up very early and would work until eleven or eleven-thirty. Very few people could come into this room, and I was amongst them. I would walk very quietly. The rest of the day Hemingway would spend his time . . .

(Cut to Sergio remembering, as Guide rambles on, what the village was like years ago.

Camera cuts to old stills of Cuban poverty.)

SERGIO *(voice over)*:   His name is René Villarreal. Hemingway found him when he was a little boy playing in the streets of San Francisco of Paula.
I read that somewhere.
He molded him to his needs.
The faithful servant and the great lord.
The colonialist and Gunga Din.

Hemingway must've been unbearable.
This was his refuge, his tower, his island in the tropics.

(Cut to the present House—books upon books, the bar still set up, more rifles and ski equipment.)

SERGIO *(voice over)*: Boots for hunting in Africa, American furniture, Spanish photographs, magazines and books in English, a bullfight poster.
Cuba never really interested him.
Here he could find refuge, entertain his friends, write in English, and fish in the Gulf Stream.

(Cut to Sergio hiding behind partition as tourist group leaves, with the Guide still talking.)

GUIDE: In 1947 many people and journalists came to see Hemingway, to interview him. They never left him in peace to write in this room. She thought that by building that study he would be able to isolate himself. She had ten windows put in so the air could circulate and he could enjoy himself.

(Cut to Sergio peeking out of the window, Elena far across the grounds.

Cut to Elena calling.)

ELENA: Sergio!

(Cut back to Sergio ducking out of sight at the window for a moment. He then stares out the window; and she, at last resort, hitches a ride back to town with one of the tourists.)

ELENA: Wait a minute!

(Cut back to Sergio watching Elena's departure. He can now relax.

Cut to Lecture Hall.)

(SCREEN TITLE): ROUND TABLE. LITERATURE AND UNDERDEVELOPMENT.

(Cut to Speaker's Panel on the dais.)

RENÉ DEPESTRE*: Culture, in an underdeveloped country, is the sometimes painful and costly operation by which people become conscious of their ability to change their social life, to write their own history, and to choose the best of their traditions in order to make them bear fruit through the conditions created by the struggle for national liberation.

EDMUNDO DESNOES: We were just a few steps away from the Negro cooks and servants of the school. I discovered I was a spy, a derogatory term used in order to look down on Latin Americans. I know now that although I look white, Anglo-Saxon, and Protestant, I really am a southern Negro. All Latin Americans are Negroes, discriminated against, oppressed, rejected, ignored, strangers in this new swindle which has pretensions of universality. The American way of life, the great white dream of the United States.

GIANI TOTI†: Now it's the turn of the devil's advocate, he who piles doubt upon doubt and who asks you: But, sirs, don't you realize that the words you are using—underdevelopment, under-development—are sick, or at least sickly? Don't you realize that these words might be language-traps, accomplices of an already wasted culture, a stratagem, a linguistic alibi, a linguistic-ideological arrangement, that might lead us to the mental peace of formulas?

(Cut to Sergio in the audience following the line of argument.)

---

* Depestre is perhaps Haiti's best living writer. He now lives in Cuba.
† An Italian novelist.

TOTI: It is useless to flee from the linguistic continent of underdevelopment and forget that the basic contradiction of our times is not the contradiction between North American imperialism and the three underdeveloped continents, but the contradiction between the impetuous development of the productive forces of all the world and the forms and the relations of the production of capitalism, between the socialist revolution and the capitalist system in its last imperialistic phase.

(Cut back to the Panel.)

DAVID VIÑAS*: For example, you speak of the basic contradiction between the proletariat and capitalism. I believe that what you have said is entirely abstract. The basic contradictions are verified in the reality and when the basic contradiction is embodied it is transmitted into war. For me, at this moment, the basic contradiction is not to be found between the European proletariats and capitalists, but in an area where the war embodies, materializes, and shows what the basic contradiction is; in other words, Vietnam.

(Cut to Sergio in the audience, listening, smoking, doodling. Everybody is bored and restless. The debate seems to make no sense.)

TOTI: This discussion is based only on the fact if the basic contradiction is the one or the other.

VIÑAS: No, no, no . . .
On a level derived exclusively from Marxist scholastics, I do agree with you, but in the concrete embodiment I see it as something else.

(Cut to Desnoes, dressed in suit and tie. He lights a cigar and puffs from time to time.)

* An Argentine novelist.

SERGIO (*voice over*): What are you doing up there with that cigar? You must feel pretty important. Here you don't have much competition.

Outside of Cuba you'd be a nobody . . .

But here, you're well situated.

Who's seen you, and who can see you now, Edmundo Desnoes?

(*Cut to the audience, a member of which has his hand up.*)

PANEL MAN: Your name, please?

AN AMERICAN: Jack Gelber.*

(*Cut to Desnoes, translating Gelber's remarks into Spanish.*)

DESNOES: Jack says that if the Cuban Revolution is an original revolution, why does it use conventional means like round tables, and why doesn't it develop a more dynamic method of establishing a relationship between the panel and the public.

(*Cut to the highway. Sergio is in the distance, walking across toward the camera. Camera zooms in very slowly to close up on him, as he speaks voice over, so close he becomes a terrible blur.*)

SERGIO (*voice over*): I don't understand. The American was right. Words devour words and they leave you in the clouds.

A thousand miles away.

How does one get rid of underdevelopment?

It marks everything. Everything.

What are you doing down there, Sergio?

What does all this mean?

You have nothing to do with them.

You're alone.

In underdevelopment nothing has continuity, everything is for-

---

* The American playwright whose works include *The Connection* and *The Cuban Thing*. Gelber wrote the introduction to the American edition of *Inconsolable Memories*.

gotten. People aren't consistent.
But you remember many things, you remember too much.
Where's your family, your work, your wife?
You're nothing, you're dead.
Now it begins, Sergio, your final destruction.

(Cut to the foyer in Sergio's apartment building. He opens his mailbox, withdraws two letters, and opens one. Inside, a stick of chewing gum and a razor blade are enclosed.)

SERGIO *(voice over)*: Every time my old lady writes it's the same thing. She knows I don't chew gum and that I use an electric shaver.
The only thing I've asked her for are books and magazines.
I can't read her handwriting.
They're crazy.
We don't understand each other.

*(Cut to Sergio leaving the building.
He walks down the street.*

Cut to the schoolyard. Huge sign over the main building identifies this as the Lenin School. Girls in school attire come out. Sergio watches the young girls.)

(SCREEN TITLE): HANNA.

(Cut back to the school yard. It is now a Catholic school, fifteen years earlier. A beautiful young blonde girl emerges, meets Sergio, and they run off, holding hands.)

SERGIO *(voice over)*: Hanna is the best thing that has ever happened to me. Running away from Hitler, they landed in Cuba.

(Cut to Sergio and Hanna playing in bed together.

A series of cuts follows—to the woods, where they make love; to a rapid succession of still photos of Sergio and Hanna together in New York; to a furniture store opening, complete with the ceremonial cutting of ribbon, a benediction by a priest, and champagne cocktails; to Sergio working at his desk late at night; to Sergio driving alone along the Malecon; to a coffee shop with him and Hanna. Eventually she leaves him, touching him on the shoulders only.)

SERGIO *(voice over):*   Hanna was more mature, more of a woman than the underdeveloped girls here.

How long were we together?

I can't remember.

It's the best thing that has ever happened to me.

Why did I let her go?

Why didn't I run after her?

When she left for New York with her parents we were going to be married.

We didn't believe in formalities but we thought it would be best. We had plans. I was going to go to New York, make my life with her. I wanted to be a writer and she believed in me.

She believed in me.

She was going to help me.

Then my father gave me a furniture store.
I buried myself behind a desk.
I worked like mad for two years.
"Hanna, darling, I can't leave now. Please understand. I don't
want to go there with empty hands . . ."
Hanna, darling.
One day it was too late.
I'll always look for you.
Where are you now?
What do you think of me now?

*(Cut to Sergio riding in a taxi in a driving rain. The cab slowly
approaches Sergio's apartment building. He spots Elena and
stops the cab short.)*

SERGIO: Wait, stop; stop right here.

*(Cut to Sergio dashing to the apartment's garage entrance to
avoid Elena. She sees him and gives chase.)*

ELENA: Sergio! Sergio!

(Cut to Sergio's balcony. He looks out over the city. The doorbell rings. He ignores it. The bell keeps ringing. Sergio moves back into the apartment and turns on the television, silently. We see on the TV a close-up of a newsreel from the southern U.S. civil rights struggle. The doorbell continues to ring. Finally he answers.

Cut to Sergio's living room couch, the next day. A Militiaman and a Militiawoman are asking Sergio a series of questions. They write on camera, as he answers the questions off camera. As the Militiaman asks the questions, the Militiawoman looks around the apartment in scornful contempt at Sergio's relative opulence.)

MILITIAMAN: Head of the family. Surname . . . ?
Second surname?

SERGIO: Bendoiro.

MILITIAMAN: Name?

SERGIO: Sergio.

MILITIAMAN: Occupation?

SERGIO: None.

MILITIAMAN: You don't work?

MILITIAWOMAN: How do you live?

SERGIO: From the rent of several apartments.

MILITIAMAN: An ex-landlord . . .
Age?

SERGIO: Thirty-eight years old.

MILITIAMAN: Total income?

SERGIO: 600 pesos.

MILITIAMAN: Income from other members of the family?

SERGIO: I live alone.

MILITIAMAN: Do you pay the Urban Reform?

SERGIO: No.

MILITIAMAN: The last month you paid?

SERGIO: I've never paid anything.

MILITIAMAN: General occupation: owner, acquirer, illegal usage . . .

SERGIO: Owner.

MILITIAMAN: Any embargo?

SERGIO: No.

MILITIAMAN: Approximately how many square meters? More or less.

MILITIAWOMAN: It's pretty big.

MILITIAMAN: Yes. Shall we say 100 or 200?

SERGIO: Would you like to measure it?

MILITIAMAN: No. I'll take your word. Let's say 300. If that's not right we'll change it afterwards.
Type of construction: bricks . . .
It's one apartment.
How many rooms?

SERGIO: A bedroom and a study

MILITIAWOMAN: Servant's quarters?

SERGIO: Two.

MILITIAMAN: How many toilets?

SERGIO: Five.

MILITIAMAN: How many baths?

SERGIO: Three.

MILITIAMAN: Elevators? Two. State of upkeep? Good. Sign here . . .

SERGIO: And what's all this for?

MILITIAMAN: We're just verifying.

SERGIO: Yes, but . . .

MILITIAMAN: Don't worry. If there's anything wrong we'll let you know.

SERGIO: All right . . .

(Cut to Sergio in taxicab driving around Havana. The cab attempts to turn, and a policeman approaches.)

POLICEMAN: Hey wait! You can't turn there . . .

SERGIO: We're going two more blocks . . .

POLICEMAN: Go straight ahead.

SERGIO: I'll get off here.

(Cut to Sergio walking along the street. He runs into a pro-government student demonstration.)

SERGIO *(voice over)*:   In the midst of all this I'm living off rents. I still have thirteen, no, twelve, eleven years to collect. It's been two years since they took away my apartment house.

(Cut to student procession passing.)

SERGIO *(voice over)*:   Everything comes to me either too early or too late. Before, I might've been able to understand what was going on here. Now, I can't.

(Cut to opening "credits" scene at carnival. The scene now continues silently as Sergio talks on.)

SERGIO *(voice over)*:   I'm thirty-eight years old and I'm already an old man. I don't feel wiser or more mature. Rotted away, but more stupid.
Like a piece of rotten fruit.
Like refuse.
It might have something to do with the tropics.
Here everything matures and rots easily.
Nothing endures.

(Cut to Sergio continuing to walk, his jacket now off, his tie now loosened; a tacky photographer takes his picture.

Cut to Sergio's apartment. He is at home now, looking through an old scrapbook of stills—his childhood on the beach, with the priest, his marriage, a passport photo.)

SERGIO *(voice over)*:   I'm an old man already. I've been in whorehouses since I was thirteen. When I was fifteen I thought I was a genius.
At twenty-five I owned an elegant store.
Then Laura.
My life is like a monstrous vegetable with large leaves without fruit.
I think I affect a certain dignity.

(Cut to Sergio's apartment doorway. The door is open and an angry Elena's brother is at the door. He pushes his way into Sergio's room.)

ELENA'S BROTHER: You're Sergio?

SERGIO: Yes.

BROTHER: I'm Elena's brother.

SERGIO: Is she sick?

BROTHER: She's never sick. It's something else. She says you took advantage of her.

SERGIO: It isn't like that . . .

BROTHER: You've ruined her and that's got to be fixed.

SERGIO: What?

BROTHER: This is not something that can be paid for with dresses.
She says you promised to marry her and then you took advantage of her.

SERGIO: That I promised . . . ? It isn't like that.

BROTHER: I don't know if it is or not!

(Cut to a restaurant. Sergio, Elena, and her brother sit at a table. The brother is angry, Elena and Sergio contrite. A crowd looks on.)

SERGIO *(voice over)*: Elena would do anything. I should've known that. I didn't want any trouble with the police. I was willing to marry her if she wanted. I was afraid.

BROTHER: Tell him what you told Mother.

ELENA: You deceived me!

SERGIO: What?

ELENA: You deceived me.

SERGIO: Why?

ELENA: You said you were going to give me some of your wife's dresses, and then you took advantage of me.

SERGIO: If you say so . . . But you know it isn't true. Besides, you're not a virgin.

BROTHER: You are being disrespectful!

SERGIO: Look.

BROTHER: I know my sister's no whore, dammit!

(Cut to the street outside of the restaurant.)

SERGIO *(voice over)*:   How could I get mixed up in all this?
I resigned myself.
I was going to let myself be dragged through to the end.
I was afraid.

(Cut to Elena's parents now joining them outside the restaurant.)

ELENA'S MOTHER: Girls must go to the altar as virgins: That's the greatest treasure a woman can give in marriage.

SERGIO: Now women are liberated.

BROTHER: Don't start talking as if you were a revolutionary, because you're not!

MOTHER: My daughter is not liberated.

FATHER: If you don't marry her, I'll . . .

BROTHER: Keep quiet!

FATHER: It's your fault!

BROTHER: What?

SERGIO: If I marry her it's because I want to.
You're not going to force me into it!

FATHER: Nobody can make fun of my daughter!

BROTHER: Be quiet!

ELENA: Why didn't you want to see me? Did you want to get rid of me?

SERGIO: It isn't that. I'll marry you. I've got to think.

ELENA: Think what?

SERGIO: I've got to get the permit, don't I? I've got to get my divorce papers.

MOTHER: You're divorced?

SERGIO: Yes, I'm divorced.

FATHER: You'll have to marry her!

BROTHER: Why did you bring her?

MOTHER: That night she came home late. She told me. She came home with her panties stained with blood . . .

SERGIO: That's not true!

(Cut to Elena's family leaving the scene in a taxicab.)

SERGIO *(voice over)*: I was sure that she was not a virgin. Poor devils!
What could they get out of all this?

(Cut to the police station. The Desk Sergeant types Sergio's answers to the questions.)

OFFICER: Do you have anything to explain?

SERGIO: It isn't true. I have had relations with her, but they were voluntary. There was no abuse and certainly no rape. All that is a lie.

OFFICER: Sign here, Sergio.

(Cut to Sergio taking his place on a bench with some down-and-outers. He takes out a cigarette to smoke, offers one to the man sitting next to him, and eventually to all around.

Cut to Sergio entering courtroom. Camera pans members of the Court, while the Bailiff is heard, voice over.)

BAILIFF: The accused, Sergio Carmona Bendoiro, planned to seduce Elena Josefa Dorado, age sixteen, and to that effect took her to his apartment located at Linea, Vedado, where he abused her virginity although knowing that said young girl was mentally disturbed and therefore incapable of resisting.

LAWYER: Do you have anything to say?

SERGIO: Yes.

LAWYER: Answer the prosecutor.

PROSECUTOR: Do you know Elena Josefa Dorado?

SERGIO: Yes.

LAWYER: When you answer, look at the judge.

SERGIO: Sorry. Yes, sir.

PROSECUTOR: Where did you meet her?

SERGIO: On Twenty-third Street, in Vedado.

PROSECUTOR: Is it true that you took her to your apartment and had sexual intercourse with her?

SERGIO: Yes.

PROSECUTOR: Tell me, before the night in question, did the plaintiff confess to you whether she had had sexual intercourse with another man?

SERGIO: No, never.

SERGIO *(voice over)*: I was the only one who spoke with some coherence.

That finished me.

They treated me as if I had cheated some "unfortunate common person."

ELENA: Yes, also to give me some dresses he . . . offered me. Those that belonged to his wife who had gone North.

SERGIO *(voice over)*: Now everything is "the people." Before, I would have been the respected one and they the damned guilty ones.

MOTHER: She had these black and blue marks, and she told me that this man . . .

(Cut to the Mother physically attacking Sergio; she has to be pulled off by policemen.)

MOTHER: The bastard, he has nerve . . .

LAWYER: Did you threaten Sergio's life?

FATHER: Yes, if he didn't marry her.

LAWYER: You threatened him?

PROSECUTOR: What did Sergio say?

FATHER: He said that he would get the permit, but in the end he didn't marry her.

PROSECUTOR: When did they take Elena to the doctor?

BROTHER: I don't know exactly. My mother says she took Elena some months before all this happened.

PROSECUTOR: Do you know what the doctor said?

BROTHER: No.

PROSECUTOR: And the results of the tests . . . ?

SERGIO *(voice over)*: Then came the verdict.

(Cut to the verdict being read voice over. We watch the court in action—closing arguments made, judges conferring and passing judgment, the courtroom filing out.)

BAILIFF: The accused, Sergio Carmona Bendoiro, invited Elena Josefa Dorado, age sixteen, for a walk on the evening of the 25th of January, 1962, and during said walk they went to the home of the accused located at Linea Street, where they had sexual intercourse.

According to tests performed, there is no proof that Elena Josefa Dorado shows any signs of mental disturbance nor that she was insane or unconscious at that time.

Secondly: The district attorney has sustained his conclusions as definite, and they have been duly recorded in folio 6 and 7.

Thirdly: The defense sustained as definite its conclusions in which it concretely denied every charge placed by the district attorney, pleaded the acquittal of the accused and the absolvement from court costs.

Finally: In the facts proved as true, there are no grounds to sustain the crime of rape as charged by the district attorney. Due to the above and executing articles 142, 240, 741, and 742 of the Social Defense Code and the Criminal Prosecution Law, we render the following verdict:

We hereby absolve the accused of the crime of rape as charged by the district attorney.

(Cut to Sergio and the Defense Attorney embracing. Sergio leaves the courtroom, relieved.)

SERGIO *(voice over)*: It was a happy ending, as they say. For once, justice triumphed.

But was it really like that?
There is something that leaves me in a bad position.
I've seen too much to be innocent.
They have too much darkness inside their heads to be guilty.
I hope they haven't shut her up.

(Cut to Sergio's apartment. He is in pajamas. He goes to pick up newspapers slipped under the door. The camera jumps across the newspaper as Sergio's "eyes.")

(NEWSPAPER):   MORE PLANES AND BATTLESHIPS TO FLORIDA.
KENNEDY RETURNS SUDDENLY TO WASHINGTON.
YOUNG MOTHER GIVES BIRTH TO TRIPLETS.
DOG WITH TWO HEARTS.
TRADE UNIONS COMPETE IN PROFITS.
BULLETIN-BOARD MATERIAL. POST IT WHERE YOU WORK. CUT OUT AND PASTE.
HOW TO PREVENT TETANUS.
VACCINATION IS THE ONLY SURE PROTECTION.
WORDS OF MAO TSE-TUNG.
Trying to solve ideological problems and the problem of what is right or wrong through administrative regulations or by repressive methods is not only useless but also harmful.

(Cut to Sergio with Noemí. She gives him a packet of photos. They are of her baptism.)

SERGIO *(voice over)*:   She brought me a stack of photographs.
They were taken when she was baptized.
It wasn't like I thought it would be.
It's nothing.
The clothes didn't cling to her body.
There were lots of people.
I hadn't thought about them.

Witnesses who are always everywhere.

(Cut to Sergio lying on his bed, daydreaming of making love to Noemí.

Cut to close-up of John F. Kennedy.)

(SCREEN   TITLE):   ᐧOCTOBER   22,   1962—KENNEDY
SPEAKS.

*(Cut to aircraft carriers, newspaper stills, aerial reconnaissance
shots, and maps of Cuba, as Kennedy is heard, mutedly, in
background, in his address to the United States announcing the
sighting of missiles in Cuba and military preparations for the
blockade of the island.*

Cut to Havana streets. Campesinos, *artists*, milicianos, *all are
preparing for the coming crisis.)*

KENNEDY: I have directed . . . initial steps to be taken immediately . . . a strict quarantine on all offensive military equipment . . . continued and increased close surveillance of Cuba
and its military build-up. . . . It shall be the policy of this nation
to regard any nuclear missile launched from Cuba as an attack
by the Soviet Union on the United States, requiring full retalia-
tory response upon the Soviet Union. . . . Now your leaders are
no longer Cuban leaders. . . . They are puppets and agents of an
international conspiracy. . . . Your lives and lands are being
used as pawns by those who deny you freedom. . . .

SERGIO *(voice over):*   What's all this for?
What are they going to get out of it?

*(Cut to Sergio walking along, staring uncertainly. Havana is
mobilizing. Jeeps and armored cars occupy the streets.)*

SERGIO *(voice over):*   And if it all started right now?
It's no use protesting.
I'll die like the rest.
This island is a trap.
We're very small, and too poor.
It's an expensive dignity.

(Cut to Fidel Castro on television. As he talks, we watch Havana becoming an armed camp. More milicianos, billboards with calls to action, anti-aircraft batteries being set up.)

FIDEL CASTRO: We shall acquire whatever weapons we feel like acquiring, and we shall take the measures we consider necessary to guarantee our defenses. Which ones? There's no reason why we should tell the imperialists. No one is going to inspect our country. No one is going to come to inspect our country, because we grant no one the right. We will never renounce the sovereign prerogative that within our frontiers we will make all the decisions and we are the only ones who will inspect anything. Anyone intending to inspect our country should be ready to come in battle array. If they blockade our country they will exalt our nation because we will resist. They threaten us by saying we'll be nuclear targets. We are part of humanity and we run the necessary risks, yet we are not afraid. We have to know how to live during the age we happen to live in, with the dignity to know how to live; every man and woman, young and old, we are all one in this hour of danger, and it is the same for all of us, revolutionaries and patriots, and victory shall be for all. Our country or death! We shall win!

(Cut to the Malecon as water cascades up the rocks and across the highway as Sergio walks in deep thought.

Cut to water and soap going down sink drain as Sergio finishes washing.

Cut back and forth, from Sergio passing the time in his apartment, to Havana preparing to fight. Sergio watches the moon through his telescope, then throws himself on his bed. Meanwhile, tanks are revving up. Sergio plays with his cigarette lighter, flicking it on and off. Soldiers are setting up their artillery.

Cut to Havana seen from Sergio's apartment. Now it is dawn. The camera pans Havana and the harbor, down to the Malecon. Camera zooms in on aircraft batteries being hoisted onto a nearby roof; again pans the Malecon, closing up as tanks roll along. The noise of the sea combined with the rumble of the tanks becomes louder and louder and louder.)

Lucia 196– (Part III)
(1969)

About *Lucia*

Fidel Castro, in his speech to the Cuban Federation of Women in late 1966, declared: "And if someone asks us what is the most revolutionary thing the Revolution is doing, it is this: the Revolution which is taking place in the women of our country."

Indeed, the Cuban woman has historically been the most oppressed of that oppressed nation. Only a month after coming to power, in February 1959, the Cuban leader had said, "The whole world knows about the tragedy which confronts women and Blacks. These are the two sectors most discriminated against. We talk a lot about racial discrimination, which is true. But no one talks about sexual discrimination." And in Cuba then, as in the United States today, it was the Black woman who was the most oppressed of all.

The story of Cuban women, like that of oppressed peoples everywhere, however, was not a story of the suffering alone, but of struggle against that suffering. In the long war of independence from Spain, women played a prominent part. Rosa the Bayamesa, a slave who became a captain in the liberation army (like Harriet Tubman, who became a general in the Union Army and "conducted" the Underground Railway to the north), was noted for her courage in the face of danger. Women fought together with men against North American intervention and the succession of dictatorships which followed the defeat of Spain. In the Sierra and in the cities of Cuba, Haydee Santamaría, Melba Hernández, Clementina Serra, Vilma Espin, Celia Sánchez,* and hundreds of others played a major role in making the Cuban Revolution. Today that revolution touches every Cuban woman.

In the literacy campaign, 56 per cent of those who became literate were women. Now, a decade later, half the elementary students and more than half of the secondary students are girls. Over 40 per cent of the students in higher education are women: in science, 50 per cent; architecture, 60 per cent; medicine, 50 per cent; biology and biochemistry, 60 per cent.

In a country characterized by its *machismo*, the women's federation now numbers 1.3 million members, over half the island's women over fourteen years of age. The federation has seen its first task as getting women into productive work, liberating them from the home. In 1958, an estimated 194,000 women were doing such work; in 1970, the figure rose to 600,000. By 1975, there will be a million working Cuban women. Today 20

* Haydee Santamaría and Melba Hernández were the only two women participants in the July 26, 1953, attack on the Moncada barracks. Haydee is today the director of the Casa de las Americas publishing house; Melba is the head of the Cuban Committee for Solidarity with the Indochinese Peoples, and an officer in the armed forces. Clementina Serra, a leader of the former Popular Socialist Party, now directs the infant nursery system. Vilma Espin and Celia Sánchez were among the very first women to join the *Granma* survivors in the hills. Vilma is now president of the Federation of Women; Celia is first secretary in the Prime Minister's office. All are members of the Central Committee of the Communist Party.

per cent of the industrial work force and 50 per cent of those in light industry are women.*

To accomplish this "revolution in the revolution" numerous new laws and institutions have been developed: abortion is now legal, though not encouraged; birth control devices are also available; free medical care has been accompanied by a possible six-month paid maternity leave; divorce is easily obtainable, marriage no longer forced. Perhaps most important is the system of child care centers and kindergartens, which cover the country, allowing working women to leave their children (from forty-five days to six years of age) to be cared for, fed, and bathed, for hours or days, depending on job circumstances. Agricultural workers, for example, may go to a distant field camp for a week at a time. In fact, Cuban leaders have reported that only with massive women's participation could the large-scale agricultural diversification brought by the Revolution be accomplished.

With a major role in producing the wealth of the country, women have been playing a corresponding political role. More than 100,000 women each year are enrolled in political studies. Over half the members of the Committees for the Defense of the Revolution are women; and 50,000 women are CDR guards. In 1969, hundreds of thousands of women gave 20 million hours of voluntary labor in agriculture, services and industry.

Prior to the Revolution, says Fidel, "from the daughters of the humblest families went forth a great legion to serve in the houses of the rich, to work in the bars, to earn a miserable living in the houses of prostitution." Women were seen as objects of pleasure, as ornaments. Even in the upper classes, most women could not finish their studies. Women were prepared by society for marriage. Today, a major occurrence of divorce (the writer does not mean to give the impression of an epidemic of divorce; in fact, the rate is low compared to the United States)

* Indeed, the Minister of Light Engineering is a woman.

comes when one partner is a revolutionary and the other is not. The revolutionary, often as not, is the woman.

In his visit to Chile in 1971, Fidel told a press conference, "I believe we are in for a long struggle. However, the fundamental role in the liberation of women must be played by the women themselves through their incorporation into the process, into the struggle."

It is this sense of women intervening in their own destinies that provides the theme for *Lucia*. Running a full two and a half hours, *Lucia* tells the stories of three women at different points of Cuban history: 1895 and the war for independence; 1933 and the overthrow of the Machado dictatorship; and 196–, the year left purposely vague.

The epic production is the first full-length work by director Humberto Solás (shown at left), twenty-six years old at the time of filming. He was seventeen when the Revolution came to power. Although he had studied to be an architect, he entered ICAIC upon its formation. After scripting and directing a number of short documentaries, he made *Manuela*, about a young woman who comes of age as a *guerrillera* in the Sierra. That was 1966 and the following year Solás began *Lucia*. That Cuba's foremost young director, a man, should choose to make his first two films about the revolutionary awakening of Cuban women testifies to the effect of that awakening on Cuban men.

Lucia 1895 portrays a woman of that Cuban landowning class whose own national interests gave rise to the independence movement against Spain. Lucia's family is anti-Spanish and patriotic. Raised almost like a nun in conditions not far from serfdom, Lucia approaches middle age still a virgin. She falls deeply in love with a Spanish adventurer, later to discover that he is an espionage agent for the colonial government. Inadvertently she betrays her revolutionary brother, who is massacred with his comrades by Spanish mercenaries. In a crowded town plaza, Lucia rushes at her ex-lover, now wearing a Spanish officer's uniform, and stabs him to death.

That is the plot synopsis, and Solás dazzles the viewer with an emotional force that overwhelms. Performed in a style touched by the flamboyance of the period, this segment plays almost like opera. Solás himself has acknowledged the Visconti influence in re-creating the romantic culture that dominated that historical period, and more than one reviewer has credited the young Cuban with outdoing the Italian. The sequence where machete-wielding Cubans, riding naked on horseback, do battle with Spanish troops, says the Canadian film magazine *Take One*, "communicates an animal fury that makes the terminal carnage of *The Wild Bunch* look like stock Hollywood heroics." Jorge Herrera's camera work presents such a heightened bravura that the viewer becomes caught up in the film. That photography, combined with the staging and editing, makes the written script of *Lucia 1895* absolutely inadequate in conveying a sense of the film. Some have argued that the episode is too long. To which England's *Sight and Sound* reviewer replies with a quote from Picasso to a woman who complained that a Cézanne painting of a man in a white shirt had one arm longer than the other: "Madam, an arm as well painted as this one can never be too long."

Lucia 1933 is the alienated daughter of a Cuban businessman. Her contempt for the corruption of that class leads her to fall in love with a young revolutionary and follow him into the struggle. Soon she is a revolutionary in her own right, organizing her women co-workers in a clothing factory and participating in the general strike. With the downfall of the Machado dictatorship the new Republic remains bourgeois and corruption becomes rampant. Lucia's mate, frustrated at the "uncompleted" revolution, becomes involved in a futile individual action against the new regime and is killed. Lucia still has her memories, but more than those she has a new way of life based on her commitment to struggle. Solás has said that this is his favorite of the three *Lucia* episodes. Contrary to the stunning extremes of the first part, the camera here uses muted tones; whereas the first Lucia is played Magnani-like by Raquel Revuelta, this Lucia is a controlled subtlety in the hands of Eslinda Núñez (Noemí in *Memorias*). The effect is a pastiche suggestive of Hollywood of the period portrayed. It was perhaps this episode that led King Vidor to argue that *Lucia* was the one truly

great film of the 1969 Moscow Film Festival, where it won the Gold Medal.

Lucia of the 1960s is, like her historical namesakes, a creature of her time, but now the time is one of Revolution in power. Work and education are necessary to consolidate and build upon the new gains. But Lucia finds that her newlywed husband, a self-proclaimed "revolutionary," intends that never will she work, study, or do anything but serve his needs. Lucia is supported by and draws strength from the community of newly emancipated men and women—especially the women—in toppling this household czar. The two are played by Adela Legrá and Adolfo Llauradó, who also starred as the couple in Solás' *Manuela.*

The outcome remains ambiguous as the struggle against *machismo* continues. This may not be the most satisfying ending to women of our society who are themselves genuinely involved in a movement which has to work at a different level. But the portrayal of the Cuban level seems accurate enough. Solás says the episode is about "the contradiction between a world that is avant-garde and radical in conception and an everyday morality that is archaic and full of preconceived ideas." Solás' attempt here—and obviously the Revolution's ongoing task—is to sharpen that contradiction so as to eliminate the latter. The revolution performs its task by hard work and audacity. Solás directs here with great glee and abandon as Tomás, the oppressive husband, becomes a buffoon with his male supremacy. Standing out as he does in bold relief obviously serves Solás' pedagogical purposes. Refrains to the tune of *Guantanamera* provide a running commentary not so much Brechtian as in the Afro-Cuban tradition.* Tomás is no less, and perhaps more, of

---

* From the African culture in Cuba's history comes the *guaguaco* and from the Cuban peasant the *decimas*, two different musical forms which allow for the improvisation of verses and are both used popularly, along lines similar to calypso.

a male supremist than Sergio in *Memorias*. But unlike Sergio, Tomás' future is cast with the Revolution. That, together with his newly revolutionary wife, give him the possibility of liberation from his archaic ideas.

Credits

Script*:	Humberto Solás
	Julio García Espinosa
	Nelson Rodríguez
Director:	Humberto Solás
Director of photography:	Jorge Herrera
Produced by:	Raúl Canosa
Editor:	Nelson Rodríguez
Sound engineers:	Ricardo Istueta
	Carlos Fernández
Music:	Leo Brower
Costumes:	María Elena Molinet

The film was produced on black-and-white 35-mm. film and runs 160 minutes (1968)

Cast:

Adela Legrá (*Lucia*)

Adolfo Llauradó (*Tomás*)

* The translation is by Susan North, who lent invaluable assistance in preparing the Cuban Film Festival and in its aftermath. The translation is not altogether literal, but does attempt to capture the idiomatic flavor of Cuban slang.

LUCIA 196— (PART III)

(It is very early morning, somewhere in Oriente Province. Two peasant women are sitting by the edge of the road, chatting. It is chilly and the women have wrapped towels around their heads. A farm truck comes noisily down the road. It is full of women who are singing a saucy nonsense folk song: "Oh, manengue,* *we peasant women neither sell ourselves nor do we give ourselves away for free, oh,* manengue." *The truck stops to pick up the two women. They scramble quickly up into the truck, urged on by the other women in it.)*

(Cut to three girls running out of a little house. They are straggling a bit, so the women in the truck razz them to hurry.)

(Cut to the truck approaching a little cluster of huts. It stops in front of a very unassuming one. No one comes out.)

(Cut to the driver honking the horn.)

DRIVER: Let's see how long it takes her today. Since she's got a boyfriend we have to wake her up in the morning!

(Cut to a dark young woman, Lucia, coming out of the little house in a great hurry. She is still getting dressed, buttoning up her clothes.)

* A petty local official.

(Cut to one of the women in the truck, the eldest one and obviously the leader, shouting at Lucia.)

ANGELINA: Come on, beautiful, move it! We've waited long enough.

LUCIA: I'm coming, you barbarians!

(As the women help Lucia onto the truck, cut to Angelina.)

ANGELINA: Come on, my child, how you drag your heels! If this is the way you are now, I'd hate to see you getting up when you've got your husband lying next to you!

(All the women burst out laughing, including Lucia.)

LUCIA: What you guys don't know is that my boyfriend says that from the day we get married this one here mustn't work any more. So what can I do?

ANGELINA: What the hell are you talking about?

LUCIA: I'm telling you, he says I can't work any more!

(Angelina and the other women, all together, shout: "No, no. Let her work! She's got to work!")

(Cut to the truck going down the road.)

(Cut back to Angelina looking at Lucia, half angry and half mocking.)

ANGELINA: Listen, kid. Are you one of those little girls that gets on the truck not to go to work but to look for a husband?

(Lucia breaks out laughing.)

LUCIA: Oh, Angie! Lay off. I'm not with it this morning. It so happens that I don't feel too hot today.

(Cut to Angelina looking with surprise at an old peasant woman who rides beside her.)

ANGELINA: She says she doesn't feel too hot today!

OLD WOMAN: You don't say!

ANGELINA: I wonder who these little birds think they are.

OLD WOMAN: Must be something she ate.

LUCIA: Just a little nervous, Angie. You went through the same thing yourself, didn't you?

(The women laugh and begin to make fun of the girl.)

ANGELINA: Don't tell me you didn't!

OLD WOMAN: Go on, feed the chicken. Give him some corn. Go on! She's smart enough.

(Lucia keeps cool in the face of the mocking laughter provoked by the teasing of her companions.)

LUCIA: But everybody here has a boyfriend or is married. You all know what I'm talking about, no?

(Angelina and Old Woman continue their banter.)

ANGELINA: So she didn't get any sleep last night.

LUCIA: Okay, Angie . . .

OLD WOMAN: Look at her little eyes, how they sparkle. Just look at those eyes shine.

ANGELINA: Can you imagine what our husbands would have done to us if they caught us mixed up in a thing like this?

OLD WOMAN: O holy Jesus, just imagine!

ANGELINA: We would have been in for it.

OLD WOMAN: We would have had it for sure.

ANGELINA: We would have really gotten our ears pinned back.

(Cut to a montage of various shots of Lucia, Angelina, and the other women at work on the farm: Lucia planting seed, Angelina carrying a great jug of water, etc.)

(Cut to Lucia, her head wrapped in a towel, carrying a huge heavy bundle down the road. The road is hot and dry. A truck comes up and stops for her. The driver offers her a lift. It is Tomás, and he flirts with Lucia. She gets up into the truck. The two joke and laugh, in courtship. Against these scenes we hear, voice over, the song "Guantanamera.")

> VOICE OVER: My divine country girl
> Girl from Guantánamo
> The country is a source
> Of innumerable riches
> And beauties
> And spiritual rest.
> Men and women alike
> Must gather its bounty
> With our toil and
> Wrest from it the good things
> We want.
> The country will offer us
> Its riches freely,
> Fresh air, sunshine,
> And the pretty blush
> Of a pure and sublime love.

(The song is repeated.)

(Cut to two old peasant women gossiping and laughing in the doorway of a little house.)

FELINA: Well, what do you think of the new couple?

PIEDAD: That wasn't a wedding at all. Nothing like it.

FELINA: Oh, well then . . .

PIEDAD: And that woman, what kind of existence is that? Imagine!

FELINA: He spends the whole day on top of her.

PIEDAD: That's right. They're at it all the time.

FELINA: Listen, he doesn't even let her up for air. He won't even let her stand in the doorway . . .

PIEDAD: You don't say.

FELINA: Instead of opening the window to get a little air.

PIEDAD: But didn't you do the same thing?

FELINA: Are you kidding? Not me.

PIEDAD: When you were just married . . .

FELINA: No . . . I got to go out now and then.

PIEDAD: Not me. I got the steamroller treatment.

FELINA: Well, that was your hard luck.

(Cut to Lucia and Tomás running from one end of their house to the other. They are playing like a pair of children. Lucia hides in the wardrobe, the kitchen, etc., until Tomás finds her; then she runs to get away from him. Finally they end up in the bedroom and, inevitably, on the bed. Tomás imitates a snake and Lucia shrieks, terrified and delighted.)

(Dissolve to the newlyweds sleeping, hours later.)

(Cut to outside of the house. Two little girls come up, giggling.)

GIRL 1: Tomás! Tomás!

(Cut to interior of the house. Lucia wakes.)

LUCIA: What's going on?

(Cut back to outside and the girls. When Lucia speaks, she is off-camera.)

GIRL 1: Daddy says to tell you to come to the Community Center. It's his birthday.

LUCIA: Okay.

GIRL 1: And he says he's going to barbecue a pig.

LUCIA: Just a minute.

GIRL 2: Come on out of there! Don't stay indoors so much!

(The little girls run away, giggling.)

(Cut to the Community Center, that night. Tomás and Lucia arrive at the party. The hall is filled with people dancing, and it's very lively. Angelina and her husband Flavio, the administrator of the farm, come over to Lucia and Tomás. The two couples embrace each other, very happy. Everybody seems to have something spicy to say to the young couple. Lucia seems a little embarrassed and Tomás very proud.)

(The camera cuts to a series of shots of people dancing and celebrating.)

(Cut to Angelina, Tomás, and Lucia drinking beer at a table. Angelina has had quite a few.)

ANGELINA: Listen, Tomás . . .

TOMÁS: What, Angie?

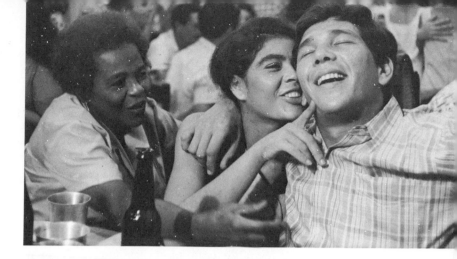

ANGELINA: What did you do to this kid that makes her look so pretty now?

(Tomás is bursting with pride.)

TOMÁS: She better tell you. She's the one that . . .

(Lucia, however, seems uncomfortable and embarrassed.)

LUCIA: Me! I don't have that kind of nerve!

(Angelina bursts out laughing in a lecherous way, and continues.)

ANGELINA: I'm sure he bit your poor little lip?

TOMÁS: Poor thing. She's bashful.

LUCIA: Come on, you guys. You're getting too fresh!

TOMÁS: Tell me, Angie, what was it that you did to Flavio?

ANGELINA: I don't know anything about it.

(Cut to Flavio and Tomás, arms around each other, passing through the dancers.)

FLAVIO: Well, now the party's over!

TOMÁS: What do you mean?

FLAVIO: Tomorrow is Monday . . .

TOMÁS: So what?

FLAVIO: . . . and you have to work. Besides, your honeymoon knocked you out . . . old man.

TOMÁS: Not me. I'm doing fine.

(The two friends laugh.)

(Cut to Angelina and Lucia sitting at the table.)

ANGELINA: Well, my little comrade, when are you coming back?

LUCIA: Back to what, Angie?

ANGELINA *(surprised)*: To what the hell do you think, to what! To work. To the farm. What else?

LUCIA *(worried)*: Oh, Angie; you are going to have to convince Tomás. He doesn't want me to work.

ANGELINA: What about the Revolution?

LUCIA: He says I have to stay home. What can I do?

ANGELINA: Can't you convince him?

LUCIA: He says that the Revolu . . . that *he's* the Revolution! I love him a lot, Angie. What am I going to do?

ANGELINA: We'll talk with him.

(Cut to a group of foreigners entering the social hall. One of the women in the group stands out particularly, as they create quite a stir among the peasants.)

(Cut to Lucia and Tomás dancing. In comes Tata, Tomás' brother. He is very drunk and very happy.)

TATA: Hey, Tomás.

TOMÁS: Hi, kid.

TATA: What's up?

TOMÁS: Just enjoying your party.

TATA: Listen, man, what are you doing to yourself? You can't go on like this. We're going to lose you!

TOMÁS: Who's gonna miss me?

TATA: Listen, man . . .

TOMÁS: Don't worry. I can take it!

TATA: Okay, you're tough, you can take it, but listen: I bet you wish you were back home right now, don't you?

(Tomás shows some annoyance. He seems to be getting tired of so much of this kind of joking.)

TOMÁS: Okay, cut it out now!

TATA: Come on, man, listen to me.

TOMÁS: Get out of here. Let me dance, will you.

TATA: All right. I'll leave you alone.

LUCIA: What's going on, baby? What's wrong?

TOMÁS: What's wrong is that these people here won't get off our backs.

LUCIA: Don't pay any attention to them, baby. You know people like to joke about newlyweds.

TOMÁS: You know something?

LUCIA: What?

TOMÁS: Tata wasn't so wrong. I wish to hell we were back home together right now, alone.

(Cut to the foreign woman, a Russian, dancing the Twist. Everyone gathers round to watch. Lucia is absorbed in watching the woman dance. A young man comes up.)

YOUNG MAN: You know how to dance this?

LUCIA: Who, me? No.

YOUNG MAN: Why don't you learn?

LUCIA: Not me! I don't know how to dance like that . . .

(Angelina and a friend are watching the foreign woman with enthusiasm.)

ANGELINA: Get a load of this one here!

WOMAN: Look at that!

ANGELINA: Really something!

WOMAN: You can say that again!

(Cut to two gossipy peasant women—from the doorway before—who are now very irritated.)

PIEDAD: Do you like this dance?

FELINA: Not me. Let's get out of here.

PIEDAD: Yeah, let's go. I don't like it either.

FELINA: Come on. Let's go.

(Cut to Flavio and Tomás in a corner of the hall. Lucia, a little ways away, is now dancing with the young man. Tomás, angry, is sweating heavily. As if he weren't having enough trouble, he also has to listen to Flavio, who is telling a story about a man with an unfaithful wife.)

FLAVIO: And that's not all, either. That afternoon when that dope Julian went out, Joey, the baker's son, went in. What a pair of horns they put on Policarpo, the husband.

(Tomás can't take any more. He leaps up, leaving Flavio with his mouth still open.)

FLAVIO: What the hell is eating you?

(Cut to Tomás, furious, approaching the center of the hall, where Lucia and the young man are dancing. He yanks the young man violently by the arm.)

TOMÁS: What the hell do you think you're doing with that woman, buddy?

LUCIA: But, Tomás . . .

YOUNG MAN: This guy is nuts.

(The young man tries to get away, but Tomás lands a punch on him. The young man responds in kind, and the fight begins. Lucia, horrified, tries to separate them. So do Flavio and Angelina. But it is useless. The two young men roll about on the floor, slugging it out.)

(Cut to the interior of Lucia and Tomás' house. It is nighttime. Lucia is sitting on the bed in tears. Tomás, as if possessed by a demon, is rushing from one window to the next, hammer in hand, nailing all the windows shut.)

LUCIA: I don't know what the hell is wrong with you! Who could have imagined it? You're supposed to be my husband, and you're acting like . . .

TOMÁS: What did you expect? That you could go around dancing to crazy music with every pair of balls that comes along?

LUCIA: But if all I was doing was . . .

TOMÁS: You're sadly mistaken . . .

LUCIA: I don't know what the hell is happening to you.

TOMÁS: Well, it's not going to be like that! You hear me?

LUCIA: But ever since we got married I don't even think about my mother. You're the only one . . .

TOMÁS: You think I'm going to stand for any of those guys that come around looking at you and wanting to dance with you and all that shit?

(Tomás drops the hammer and nails, and throws himself onto his wife on the bed.)

TOMÁS: I want you to obey me, you hear? That's what you're my wife for.

LUCIA: Okay, baby, okay.

TOMÁS: You're going to be all mine, and that's that, you hear? You're going to be only for me.

LUCIA: Okay, okay.

TOMÁS: You're going to be mine, like I want it, Goddammit!

(Lucia continues to cry. Tomás embraces her sensuously. The music of the "Guantanamera" breaks out behind a parallel montage of alternating shots of Tomás working and Lucia locked in the house. Tomás seems lively, happy, especially when he runs into one or another of the women who work at the farm. Lucia, however, doesn't know how to fill her time in her prison, and entertains herself with the most useless tasks and games, such as playing solitaire.)

VOICE OVER: The scourge of jealousy
Leads one to error.
The scourge of jealousy
Leads one to error.
It causes a ton of grief
And sufferings galore.

'Twas our grandfathers' mistake
To make the womenfolk slaves.
Only men could work and play
And enjoy themselves.
But such behavior
In our new life
Today is out of place . . .

(The song is repeated.)

(Cut to the interior of union headquarters the next day. Everybody who works at the farm has assembled here. Flavio and Angelina are chairing the meeting.)

FLAVIO: Okay, comrades. We are meeting today to hear some wonderful news: The young literacy teachers from Havana will be arriving in our town today. I want to tell you now that these young comrades are not coming here to fool around or take it easy, or any of that business. They are coming here to sweat alongside of us. They're going to help us plow, help us plant, and help us reap the fruits of our labors.

(Cut to the peasants applauding. Tomás is leaning against a column. Cut back to Flavio speaking.)

FLAVIO: So I want you to understand this. When these comrades sit down at our tables to eat with us and share our bread, they will have already earned it, and I want this clearly understood . . .

(Everybody applauds again. Cut to Angelina, who has been listening avidly to her husband's words all this time; she gets up and asks to speak.)

ANGELINA: Comrades, I want to add something. Listen, comrades, there's a rumor going round. In spite of all your clapping . . . it is still going round. We heard through the grapevine that some of our sisters who, although they support the Revolution, have said things like . . . that no sister . . . that no little skirt from Havana is going to come up here and fool around with their husbands. Well, comrades, I want you to know that this is the wrong attitude. It is not correct.

(Cut to the farmers all laughing and applauding enthusiastically. Not so Tomás.)

(Cut to the bedroom of Lucia and Tomás' house, the next morning. Tomás is asleep. Lucia comes in to wake him. Suddenly he grabs her by the hips and pulls her down into the bed.)

TOMÁS: You thought I was still asleep.

LUCIA: Ouch, stop it.

(Cut to Tomás entering the kitchen. He is humming a bolero. Lucia is making his breakfast.)

TOMÁS *(singing)*:   I dream of such beautiful things. Pretty girl, did you . . . save any coffee for me?

LUCIA: Anything you want.

TOMÁS: Anything I want?

LUCIA: And mine?

TOMÁS: A sip. Give me my coffee. I'm in a hurry.
(singing) I want you near meeeee . . .

(Cut to Tomás going into the little parlor and combing his hair in the mirror above the sideboard. Lucia comes up with the cup of café au lait.)

TOMÁS *(singing)*:   And join us in one embrace . . . and tell you . . . that we will be this way forever . . . lips to lips . . . soul to soul . . .

LUCIA: Forever?

TOMÁS: Forever . . .

LUCIA: Listen, there's something I want . . .

TOMÁS: What is it?

LUCIA: I want you to let me go see Mama.

(Close up on Tomás' face as it loses the smooth calm it had and goes cold and hard.)

TOMÁS: Look. When Belén comes to bring you the groceries, tell her to go by your mother's house to tell her to come see you here—yeah, here—and *at night*, when I'm back.

LUCIA: But darling, why are you so afraid?

TOMÁS: Baby, you don't know the people in this town. The people in this town are . . . bad.

LUCIA: You really pay attention to the people? Don't you see that they envy you?

TOMÁS: Listen, every guy in this town would like to eat you up alive, and the only one who gets to touch you around here is *me*.
(Getting up.) I've got to leave. It's late.

LUCIA: Darling, will you let me go?

TOMÁS: Listen, I never change my mind.

(Cut to the exterior of the house. Tomás comes out. On the porch there is a young man, leaning against a column. Tomás shuts the door quickly when he sees him. He approaches the young man, who is asleep. Tomás wakes him up by nudging him with his toe. The young man assembles himself quickly. Tomás goes back to the door. Lucia has looked out.)

TOMÁS: Get back in there.

(He shuts the door with a slam. He looks at the young man.)

TOMÁS: Hey, man . . .

TEACHER: Good morning.

TOMÁS: What are you doing, lying at my door?

(Tomás begins to pace anxiously back and forth on the porch. The teacher follows his footsteps.)

TEACHER: I'm the literacy teacher.

TOMÁS: So what?

TEACHER: Flavio sent me over here.

TOMÁS: So Flavio told you to come *here*?

TEACHER: Yes. Aren't you Tomás?

TOMÁS: Yeah, I'm Tomás. When did you talk to Flavio?

TEACHER: Yesterday. Yesterday afternoon.

(Tomás, very clearly displeased, pulls over a chair and sits down. He looks like he's going to lose his patience any moment.)

TOMÁS: Yesterday afternoon . . . Listen, I'm going to tell you something. The thing is that in this house . . . well, we don't need any teacher here.

TEACHER: I already know that *you* know how to read. It's your wife who doesn't.

TOMÁS: You know a lot, don't you?

TEACHER: Comrade Flavio told me to tell you that if you have any objections, you should go to see him.

TOMÁS: I think it's a good idea that we both go over to Flavio's and clear this matter up.

TEACHER: Right. That's exactly what I had in mind when I said that.

TOMÁS: Well, then, let's get going.

(Tomás gets up quickly and hurries off towards the truck. The teacher remains on the porch.)

TEACHER: Hey! Can I leave my stuff here?

TOMÁS: No. Take it all and put it on the truck. Come on, move it!

(Cut to the interior of Flavio and Angelina's house. Tomás rushes in. Angelina approaches, startled.)

ANGELINA: Hey, what's going on? Somebody sick or something?

TOMÁS: No, no, Angie. I want to speak to Flavio. Hey, Flavio, I have to talk with you.

FLAVIO: Why, what's the matter, kid?

ANGELINA: What can it be?

TOMÁS: Who sent that guy over to my place?

FLAVIO: What guy?

TOMÁS: That punk over there at the door.

(Flavio is unruffled. He and Angelina head for the door.)

FLAVIO: Let's see who it is.

ANGELINA: Oh, it's you. Come in.

(The teacher comes in. He is somewhat cowed. Flavio and Angelina go over to Tomás.)

FLAVIO: Look, Tomás. It's the teaching comrade from Havana. He's come to work so that everyone in your house can learn how to read and write properly.

TOMÁS: Yeah, but look here, who sent him over to my place, man? You know I just got married.

FLAVIO: But, so what? What's that got to do with him?

TOMÁS: Would you have liked it if they sent some guy to your house right after you got married?

ANGELINA: But what's that got to do with it?

FLAVIO: Look, Tomás; the comrade isn't going to be . . .

ANGELINA: But come on, child. What's wrong with that?

FLAVIO: . . . in your house . . . like you say . . . ALL the time. The comrade is going to work with you on the truck, and then in the evening . . .

ANGELINA: It's going to be the same in every house around here.

FLAVIO: Hold on, Tomás. And in the evening . . .

TOMÁS: Just tell me, where is he going to sleep?

FLAVIO: The comrade isn't going to be hanging around your house all the time, like you say.

TOMÁS: Oh yeah? Where is he going to sleep?

ANGELINA: In your house, Goddammit! Like in everybody else's house!

FLAVIO: You've always been a good revolutionary . . . and these are programs of the Revolutionary Government!

TOMÁS: Have it your way.

FLAVIO: And you ought to . . .

ANGELINA: But let him talk, man. Let him talk!

FLAVIO: Let me explain, Tomás. Lucia can't read, she can't write; she's a victim of Yankee imperialism . . .

TOMÁS: Yeah, whatever you say.

FLAVIO: But let me talk, Tomás. Lucia . . .

ANGELINA: Let him talk! Let him talk!

FLAVIO: This is Lucia's big chance . . . and you aren't going to stand in the way of a move that benefits everybody, and particularly your own wife.

ANGELINA: He's right.

(Tomás makes a tremendous effort to coordinate his few ideas. He looks at Flavio like a caged beast.)

TOMÁS: Listen to what I'm going to tell you. This is a program of the Revolutionary Government, right?

FLAVIO: Yes!

TOMÁS: And Lucia is a victim of Yankee imperialism, right?

FLAVIO: Right!

TOMÁS: But that guy is not going to sleep in my house!

(Tomás delivers this last line with a maximum of conviction. Flavio and Angelina lose their tempers.)

FLAVIO: Yes he *is* going to sleep in your house!

TOMÁS: And that's final.

ANGELINA: He's right, Tomás. You'll see, boy.

FLAVIO: He is going to sleep right in your Goddamn house!

TOMÁS: He is not going to sleep in my house, Angie. In my house it's me that makes the rules. I'm the boss!

FLAVIO: He's going to sleep in your house.

ANGELINA: You'll see.

(Cut to the little parlor in Tomás' house. There they sit: the teacher, Lucia, and Tomás. The young man is giving Lucia her first lessons. Tomás, sitting across the table from them, watches them with a beady eye.)

(Cut to a montage of Tomás' and the teacher at work on the farm, of Lucia learning the alphabet at night, and of the visit Angelina pays to Lucia. Tomás gives the teacher a hard time, giving him the heaviest jobs while he himself passes the time chatting with the other farmers. The young man is exhausted. In the alternating scenes, Lucia and Angelina engage in heated conversation. Angelina is trying to convince her of something. Over the scenes we hear a "Guantanamera" verse.)

VOICE OVER: Education is the most nutritious bread
For all of humankind.
Education is the most nutritious bread
For all of humankind.
The most nutritious and healthy, too
Make no mistake about it.
That's why this time all his tricks
Have failed.
Although he likes to tease
While he exploits his assistant,
At his house the visitor
Has completely succeeded.

(The song is repeated.)

(Cut to the highway. It is still daylight. Tomás and the literacy teacher are coming back from their labors at the farm. Tomás looks ironically at the young man.)

TOMÁS: Hey, buddy, you got a girl?

TEACHER: Me? Well . . . yes . . . back in Havana.

TOMÁS: But she's a lot older than you, isn't she?

TEACHER: As a matter of fact, I'm a year older than she is.

TOMÁS: No kidding. And I had always heard that all you Havana kids lived off old women.

(Tomás has said these last words in a biting manner. The teacher looks irritated.)

(Cut to the interior of Piedad's house. Piedad and Tomás go into the kitchen.)

TOMÁS: I sure need a cup of coffee. I worked pretty hard today.

PIEDAD: I got my ration today.

TOMÁS: So you got your ration.

PIEDAD: Yes, this morning.

TOMÁS: Is it weak or strong?

PIEDAD: Like you make for friends.

(The neighbor, Felina, pokes her head through the kitchen window.)

FELINA: Hello, Tomás. How are you? Since you got married you're not interested in us any more?

TOMÁS: Hi, Felina. How are you?

FELINA: Since he got hooked up he doesn't want to mix with anyone.

TOMÁS: Come on. Don't say that.

PIEDAD: Let a person talk, for God's sake.

FELINA: How's your marriage going?

TOMÁS: Fine, fine.

FELINA: That's nice. Congratulations.

TOMÁS: Thanks.

PIEDAD: That old woman is such a gossip, my God!

TOMÁS *(laughing)*: She'll hear you.

PIEDAD: So let her hear me.
You know that you had a visitor today, don't you?

TOMÁS: At my place?

PIEDAD: Our neighbor, Angelina.

TOMÁS: Angelina was in my house?

PIEDAD: She came in a truck. You know how she loves to ride around in those jalopies.

TOMÁS: What time did she leave?

PIEDAD: A little while ago. They must have had a lot to say to each other, because your wife was crying . . .

TOMÁS: Lucia?

PIEDAD: You know how sensitive she is.

TOMÁS: Okay, I have to go.

PIEDAD: You're going?

TOMÁS: Thanks for the coffee.

(Cut to the bedroom of Lucia and Tomás' house. Tomás is shaking his wife roughly by the shoulders and shouting.)

TOMÁS: Dammit, didn't I tell you that nobody comes into this house when I'm not here!

LUCIA *(in tears)*: How could I do that to Angie? I had to . . .

TOMÁS: The hell with Angie. What did she come for, dammit?

(Lucia tries to get away. He chases her around the bed until he can grab her again.)

LUCIA: She asked me to go back to work at the farm with her. And I *am* going back to the farm. I ain't gonna be locked in here all the time like this, all alone.

TOMÁS: You damn well better get this straight: The only one in this house who is always right is me. You get it?

(Tomás throws her forcefully down on the bed. She cries hysterically.)

LUCIA: You're crazy, man! You're out of your mind!

(Cut to the teacher, in the little parlor next to the bedroom. His fists are clenched.)

(Cut to the kitchen of Flavio and Angelina's house. They have just finished eating. Angelina is clearing the table.)

ANGELINA: I have to tell you something.

FLAVIO: What is it?

ANGELINA: It's about what's going on at Tomás' house.

FLAVIO: Tomás! He's a jackass! What do you expect will happen?

ANGELINA: You know, the same old thing. He won't let her work.

FLAVIO: But that's how Tomás was brought up . . . remember how his old man treated poor Felicia? And she was kept stuck in there while he was out having a good time!

ANGELINA: He treated her like a slave, but those days are gone forever.

FLAVIO: Sure, that's right.

ANGELINA: That poor woman looked like our town's own Saint Cecilia. Things really have changed, though. If that man tried to do those things now, he'd land in jail or the work farm.

FLAVIO: With or without the Revolution, nobody's gonna change that ignoramus, Tomás.

ANGELINA: Okay. But you could convince her . . .

(She reaches her hands up to Flavio's face. It seems like she wants to pick something off him.)

ANGELINA: What's that you got there? Hold still, man.

(Flavio fidgets, irritated.)

FLAVIO: No. Leave me alone. It's too hot. No, let me be, it's too hot.

(Cut to Lucia and Tomás' house. Lucia and the teacher are seated at the table. Tomás, in a nearby armchair, vigilantly watches everything that goes on. He looks like a judge.)

TEACHER: Okay, Lucia. Let's begin your first lesson.

LUCIA: My first lesson.

TEACHER: Okay, now. What's this?

LUCIA: How am I supposed to know if you don't tell me first?

TEACHER: This is called the alphabet.

LUCIA: The alph . . . and what is an alphabet?

TEACHER: The alphabet is all the letters that make up the Spanish language.

(Cut to Tomás who, in spite of his infinite jealousy, has fallen

asleep with the cigar still sticking out of his mouth. Cut back to the teacher, who comes closer to Lucia and whispers to her.)

(The ensuing scene cuts back and forth from Tomás to the teacher and Lucia.)

TEACHER: Lucia, why do you stand for such treatment?

LUCIA: What treatment? You mean from Tomás? Well, you know, he's my husband.

(Tomás wakes up, coughing. The teacher, nervous, returns to the lesson.)

TEACHER: The alphabet has twenty-eight letters and begins with the letter A.

LUCIA: A . . .

TEACHER: A . . .

(Tomás goes back to sleep. The teacher is insistent.)

TEACHER: Precisely, Lucia. Being your husband, he should be the first to respect you.

LUCIA: Yeah, but . . . well, that's just the way he is . . . and . . . I know he loves me, but . . .

(Tomás wakes up, coughing loudly. He look suspiciously at the pair, and then spits ostentatiously. Lucia and the young man are afraid that they have been caught in a "compromising" situation.)

TEACHER: The alphabet has twenty-eight letters, like I told you, and ends with the letter Z.

LUCIA: Z.

(Tomás, satisfied that nothing unusual is happening, goes back to sleep, snoring peacefully.)

TEACHER: Lucia, women are no longer slaves of their husbands.

LUCIA: But what do you expect me to do? And besides, I love him the way he is.

(Cut to the farm. It is daytime. There is a great busy movement of tractors and trucks, coming and going from the fields. A group of farmhands go by with their working tools. Flavio and Tomás come, walking alone.)

FLAVIO: Have you seen how pretty the new housing project is? Do you know the requirements?

TOMÁS: I haven't seen it, but I heard about it . . .

FLAVIO: And the first crack to get into those houses will go to families where both the husband and wife work.

TOMÁS: Well, I'll be one of the last to get into those houses, but that's okay. I'm in no hurry.

FLAVIO: I can't believe it, Tomás. You're being left behind.

TOMÁS: Look, Flavio, I'm gonna tell you something. I got my own ideas. You get me?

FLAVIO: I know that we all have our own ideas, Tomás, but you're falling behind. Like the tail of the cow, below and behind.

TOMÁS: Oh yeah?

FLAVIO: You're turning your back on reality.

TOMÁS: You think I've got my back turned on reality?

FLAVIO: It's that the times have changed, old man. You can't treat your woman as if she was a slave, like in the days of your grandfather, may he rest in peace.

TOMÁS: Look, every man paints his house the color that he wants, you know what I mean?

FLAVIO: I know that, Tomás, but you have no right to destroy Lucia's life. She's young and full of life . . .

(Tomás stops in his tracks. He is not disposed towards continuing the conversation. He speaks in a very final tone.)

TOMÁS: Look, Flavio. I do things my own way. I mind my own business because I want everybody else to mind theirs. Understood?

FLAVIO: Sure, Tomás.

TOMÁS: Well, I'm going back to work. I got a lot left to do.

(Tomás runs off towards the truck. The teacher is waiting for him there. Flavio, a bit out of breath, shouts after him.)

FLAVIO: Listen to a word of advice, man: The devil knows more because he's old than because he's a devil!

TOMÁS: Okay.

(Cut to the interior of Lucia and Tomás' house. It is the teacher's second lesson. Tomás, as always, is sitting in front of the table in his armchair. Lucia looks at Tomás and smiles. Tomás is trying to light a faulty cigar.)

LUCIA: The cigar is all discombobulated.

TOMÁS: Discombobulated?

LUCIA: I don't know what it means, but . . . I say discombobulated because . . . because the cigar's a mess.

TEACHER: Did you study yesterday's lesson?

LUCIA: Well, I think that I got something. But you get so many things in your head that you could forget some of it . . .

TEACHER: Okay. Let's review it. What is the alphabet?

LUCIA: The alphabet is . . . all the letters . . . that make up the Spanish language.

TEACHER: Very good. How many letters in the alphabet?

LUCIA: It has twenty-eight.

TEACHER: And what letter does it begin with?

LUCIA: A.

TEACHER: With the letter A. How do you write the letter A? What does it look like?

LUCIA: A little tummy and a little stick.

TEACHER: No, no. I'm going to show you how.

(The teacher gets up and stands behind Lucia. He takes the hand in which she is holding the pencil and begins to guide it over the paper.)

TEACHER: You hold the pencil like this.

(Tomás cannot believe what his eyes are seeing. He kicks the table violently.)

TOMÁS: Oh, no. Nobody ever said that to teach a girl to write you have to hold hands with her!

LUCIA: Oh, Tomás, darling, please!

TOMÁS: They never told me anything about that. How was I to know this kind of thing was going to go on right under my very nose?

TEACHER: Listen, Tomás. There's nothing funny going on here. Everybody knows that in order to teach someone to write you have to take their hand.

LUCIA: Oh, please, Tomás, for God's sake!

TOMÁS: Listen here, don't you shout at me! Don't you dare raise your voice at me! The only man who shouts in this house is me, you understand!

LUCIA: Good God, Tomás. Oh, please!

TEACHER: Look, Tomás. I'm getting a little sick of all this.

TOMÁS: I'm the one that's getting sick of this!

LUCIA: Look here, Tomás, please!

TEACHER: If you want to get me out of here, go talk to Flavio and I'll leave at once.

TOMÁS: You bet I'm gonna go talk with Flavio! You can't shout at me! *I'm* the man of this house!

(The two men are about to exchange blows. Lucia separates them, shouting.)

LUCIA: Tomás, stop it right now! The teacher will *not* leave this house!

TOMÁS: Oh, you think so?

LUCIA: What would the counterrevolutionaries think if the teacher left this house? They would think that we were like them! Well, Goddammit, I'm not going to give them that satisfaction.

(Cut to a montage of scenes showing Lucia progressively learning to read, while Tomás dogs their every footstep, spying on them through every crack and knothole he finds in the house. Over this scene we hear another "Guantanamera.")

VOICE OVER: His infinite mistrust of his wife
Won't let him understand,
His infinite mistrust of his wife
Won't let him understand,
That when she learns, he advances.
And his perpetual spying,
Which has no basis at all,

Makes him protest for no reason
Until he goes berserk
And gives way to his savage temper.

(Cut to Lucia and Tomás' bedroom. Lucia and Tomás are lying in bed. Lucia is lost in her thoughts. Tomás is finishing his cigar.)

TOMÁS: Listen, sweetheart, I'm going to give you a word of advice. Don't think so hard, you'll wear out your brain. What were you thinking about?

LUCIA: Nothing.

TOMÁS: Do you know what I was thinking about?

LUCIA: What?

TOMÁS: I was thinking about the day we met. Do you remember?

LUCIA: Of course I remember.

TOMÁS: I came along with the truck. You were walking along the highway all loaded down with a sack of *malanga*.*

LUCIA: Sweet potatoes.

TOMÁS: All right, whatever it was. The point is that you could hardly carry the damn thing. Well, then I saw you . . . I put on the brakes . . . I leaned out and I said to you . . . Do you remember what I said to you?

LUCIA: You asked if I wanted a lift.

TOMÁS: Right. And when I said that, you threw me such a look it scared me half to death. But Goddammit if the next thing I know, you were already up in the truck, sitting beside me and patting your hair and looking at me sideways. So then I says to myself, Jeeesus! What the hell have we got here! Now, I'm going to ask you one question. Why was it that you climbed into my truck so quick?

(Lucia turns her back on him. She speaks in a tone of rejection.)

LUCIA: Because I had been lugging that Goddamn thing for four hours and it was very heavy.

TOMÁS: What's the matter with you? Are you sick or something? Or are you getting a sweet tooth for Havana?

(Lucia bursts into tears.)

(Cut to the dining room that evening. We find Lucia and the teacher. The young man takes advantage of the absence of Tomás.)

TEACHER: Don't waste any more time thinking about it, Lucia. Leave now. If you don't do it now you'll never do it!

LUCIA *(tearfully)*: It's that I'm not sure. What if it turns out to be a terrible mistake?

* An edible root grown in Cuba.

TEACHER: But you can't go on living like this, locked up in these four walls and playing the servant to Tomás!

LUCIA: But I'm afraid . . .

TEACHER: Look . . .

LUCIA: Besides, I love him very much . . . and then . . .

TEACHER: All right, but look . . .

LUCIA: Maybe some day he'll . . .

(Cut to Tomás, spying on them from behind a crack in the dining room door. The scene continues from his vantage point. The teacher is insistent. He puts his arm around Lucia's shoulders.)

TEACHER: That's exactly what's making the whole thing so difficult for you. And you've just got to make up your mind . . . really . . . Lucia.

LUCIA: I know . . . I know that's true. Of course I'm going to leave. I can't go on like this . . .

(Tomás, in a fit of fury, mutters to himself.)

TOMÁS: I knew it. I knew this was going to happen! I'm going to split you in two, you son of a bitch!

(Tomás throws open the door violently. The teacher and Lucia look at him, surprised.)

TOMÁS: That's just how I wanted to catch you both, you bastards.

LUCIA: But what are you talking about, Tomás!

TOMÁS: So you just wait till the minute I leave you alone with my wife . . . you son of a bitch!

(Tomás grabs the teacher by the neck. It looks like he wants to kill him. Lucia, desperate, screams.)

LUCIA: No, Tomás! No, no!

TOMÁS: Goddammit, come over here to hold this bastard up!

LUCIA *(screaming)*: Oh my God! Stop it, Tomás, stop it!

(Tomás and the teacher begin to punch each other. Lucia runs from one side to the other, incapable of stopping them. She is screaming at the top of her lungs.)

(Cut to the interior of Flavio and Angelina's house. Someone is knocking insistently at the door. Angelina, half dressed, goes to open it. We see Lucia leaning against the doorframe. She is disheveled and her blouse is torn. She is crying miserably. Angelina brings her in and sits her down in an armchair.)

ANGELINA: Oh my God, what's the matter with this woman? Jesus, child, talk to me. Tell me, what's happened to you? Speak up. My lord, what's going on? Is it Tomás?

(Lucia, while she is crying, mumbles something that Angelina cannot understand.)

ANGELINA: Don't frighten me like this! What's the matter, my child!

(Cut to the town bar. There is nobody here but Tomás and the bartender. Tomás, with a bottle in his hand, is half singing a song. The bartender is preparing to close up the place.)

TOMÁS: . . . they gave away my kisses . . . they are killing my heart . . .

(The bartender comes over to Tomás and takes him by the arm.)

BARTENDER: Come on, we have to leave. Let's go . . .

(Tomás, completely drunk, puts up some resistance.)

TOMÁS: Where are we going?

BARTENDER: Come on. It's time to go to bed.

TOMÁS: In a little while. First we have to have a drink . . .

BARTENDER: Come on. Let's go.

TOMÁS: . . . have a little drink with me . . .

BARTENDER: No. It's time to go to bed.

TOMÁS: Just a little drink . . .

BARTENDER: Come on, brother, let's go . . .

TOMÁS: Just one.

BARTENDER: No. That's enough, now.

(The bartender has finally managed to start Tomás walking.)

TOMÁS: Okay, have it your way . . . I'm going . . .

BARTENDER: Come on, we've got to go. It's late.

TOMÁS: All right, all right. I'm going.

BARTENDER: Okay, I'll walk with you.

(Cut to Flavio and Angelina's kitchen. Lucia and Angelina are seated at the table. Lucia is drinking a cup of tea. She seems calmer.)

LUCIA: I have to get out of here this very night. If Tomás catches me, either he'll kill me or I'll kill him. This thing has got to be ended once and for all.

ANGELINA: Don't you worry. There ain't gonna be no blood spilled around here. You're going this afternoon with me . . . and you have to be tough. You've taken enough already.

(Cut to the interior of Lucia and Tomás' house. It is dawn. Tomás, drunk and shaky, comes into the house.)

TOMÁS: Lucia . . . Lucia . . .

(Tomás looks everywhere for his wife. He gets to the bedroom and throws himself on the bed. He sees a bunch of clothing tossed all over the place.)

TOMÁS: Darling, darling . . .

(Tomás begins to suspect that Lucia has left. He gets up and runs into the kitchen.)

TOMÁS: Lucia! Lucia!

(She isn't there either. He goes and sits down in the dining room. On the table, very badly scrawled, there is a note which his wife has left him. Tomás reads it out loud.)

TOMÁS: "I'm going. I'm not a slave . . ."

(Tomás, bursting with anger, gets up and runs out.)

(Cut to the street near Flavio and Angelina's house. The brakes on Tomás' truck squeal very noisily in front of the house. Tomás bangs ferociously on the horn. He shouts.)

TOMÁS: Flavio . . . Flavio . . .

(Flavio opens a window and sticks his head out.)

FLAVIO: What's going on, Tomás?

(Tomás looks at him with hostility.)

TOMÁS: Is my wife there?

FLAVIO: Your wife?

TOMÁS: Yeah, my wife!

FLAVIO: No, Tomás. We haven't seen your wife since you

married her . . . and locked her up in the house like a bird in a cage!

TOMÁS: Yeah, yeah. I know you know where my wife is. But we'll settle this matter later.

(Flavio, with a comic gesture, waves him away.)

FLAVIO: Beat it. Get lost.

TOMÁS: Yeah, later for you.

FLAVIO: He's crazy.

(Cut to the farm. Tomás pulls up in a hurry, jumps down off his truck, and intercepts a tractor which is coming along.)

TOMÁS: Hey, listen here . . .

FARMER: What's up, Tomás?

TOMÁS: Have you seen my wife?

FARMER: . . . Lucia . . . No, I haven't seen Lucia, Tomás. But I do know that a bunch of women went down to the salt flat.

TOMÁS: Over there?

FARMER: Yeah.

TOMÁS: Was it long ago?

FARMER: No. It was just a little while ago, Tomás.

TOMÁS: See you later.

FARMER: See you!

(Tomás jumps back into the truck and drives off.)

(Cut to the highway. The truck seems like a rocket, shooting down the road to the salt flat.)

(Cut to the salt flat. Tomás jumps out of the truck and begins to run. There in the distance, Lucia, Angelina, and a group of women are walking with some sacks of salt. Angelina sees Tomás coming.)

ANGELINA: Look who's coming down the road.

(Tomás runs up to the group of women. Lucia looks at him haughtily.)

TOMÁS: Put that down, and come home!

LUCIA: I'm not putting anything down.

TOMÁS: You're going to do what I say, girl!

ANGELINA: She's not going anyplace!

LUCIA: I'm not going because I don't feel like it.

TOMÁS: Let's go!

ANGELINA: Tomás, for God's sake, leave her in peace!

TOMÁS: Keep quiet, Angelina. I don't want to have to be disrespectful!

ANGELINA: I'm not keeping quiet. You have to hear her conditions!

TOMÁS: You are coming home, right now!

LUCIA: I'm not going anyplace, because I don't want to!

ANGELINA: Oh, Tomás, leave her alone already!

TOMÁS: Angelina, butt out of this. I don't want to swear at you!

ANGELINA: Let her alone!

LUCIA: That's enough of that. I'm leaving. I've had it.

(Lucia drops the sack of salt and starts to run off.)

TOMÁS: Stop right there! Stop, you bitch!

ANGELINA: Leave her alone!

(Tomás starts to run after her. Angelina and the other women run after him, trying to hold him back. Lucia runs swiftly. Tomás, still drunk, can't catch up with her. Lucia, exhausted, hides in a great mountain of salt. The women catch Tomás and hold him.)

TOMÁS: Bitch, you've ruined my life! You're going to come back home because I'm your husband, Goddammit!

LUCIA: I don't love you any more, Tomás! Go to hell! I don't love you.

(Angelina has Tomás in a full-nelson. The man, furious, tries in vain to free himself of the women.)

TOMÁS: You'll see! Let me the hell alone, Goddammit. Let go! Goddammit! Bitch!

ANGELINA: Tomás.

LUCIA: Go to hell! I never want to see you again!

TOMÁS: You're gonna come back home because I'm your husband, let me go, Goddammit! I'll kill you!

ANGELINA: Tomás!

LUCIA: Get out of here, Goddammit! Get out of here or I'll manage to kill you, you bastard!

TOMÁS: You bitch! What you deserve, Goddammit . . .

ANGELINA: Tomás!

(Cut back and forth between a series of parallel scenes of Tomás, drunk, playing hooky from work and terribly tormented, and of Lucia, melancholy and sad. Tomas is always in the town bar. Lucia is in the salt flats, but dragging herself along and listless. We hear, voice over, another "Guantanamera.")

VOICE OVER: He was under the grip
                Of a foolish anxiety,
                He was under the grip
                Of a foolish anxiety,
                A product of that jealousy
                Which comes of a poor imagination.
                Today he's missing work,
                He's morally destroyed.
                Although his wife left him
                She can't live without him.
                And as a husband he has become
                The laughing stock of the town.

(Cut to the seashore. Tomás is crying desperately among the rocks. He kicks everything that happens across his path. Lucia, on the edge of the sea, is coming home from the salt flat. She is crying. In the background there is a little girl who is coming closer. Lucia reaches Tomás. She strokes his hair.)

TOMÁS: Oh, baby, I knew you wouldn't do that to me. I love you so much. Goddammit, I knew you would change your mind.

LUCIA: I have to be useful, Tomás. If not, what do I want to live for?

TOMÁS: That's where you're wrong . . .

LUCIA: I came back because . . . because I can't live without you. But I can't stay the way you had me, Tomás. I have to work. Please understand.

TOMÁS: But if I . . .

(Tomás looks at her angrily, and pulls away from her.)

TOMÁS: Look, Goddammit. You didn't have to come all the way out here to tell me that pile of shit! You understand? To tell me that pile of shit you can keep on walking! You can go clear to hell!

LUCIA: No. I'm going to stick with you and I'm going to go work at the farm. I'm not going anywhere. I'm staying right here, because that's what I married you for.

(Tomás circles round and round his wife like a crazy person.)

TOMÁS: I love you very much, but . . . you have to obey me, do you hear? You're going to obey me, Goddammit!

LUCIA: I'm going to keep on working . . . and you're going to let me live. You're going to love me, but you're not going to abuse me any more.

TOMÁS: You've got it all wrong. You're going to toe the line, Goddammit.

(Tomás grabs her by the shoulders and throws her furiously down in the sand.)

LUCIA: Not that way! Not that way! Don't push me around, Goddammit, or I'll stop loving you, Tomás.

(The little girl whom we saw approaching before is watching the scene, alarmed.)

(Lucia and Tomás are fighting in the sand. She gets away. He runs after her until he catches her, and he throws her down in the sand again; over and over again, absurdly.)

(The little girl starts to laugh, and then she goes off, indifferent to the problems of Lucia and Tomás.)

Other Films
from Cuba

FULL-LENGTH FILMS*

THE FIRST CHARGE
OF THE MACHETE
La Primera Carga al Machete

1969. Directed by Manuel Octavio Gómez; screenplay by
Manuel Octavio Gómez, Alfredo del Cueto and Jorge Herrera;
photographed by Jorge Herrera; edited by Nelson Rodríguez;
music by Leo Brower and Pablo Milanes. With Idalia Anreus,
Eslinda Núñez, Ana Vinas and Omar Valdés. Black-and-white,
84 minutes. Luis Buñuel Prize, Venice 1969.

Manuel Octavio Gómez was born in Havana. He studied
journalism and later worked as a newspaper and television writer
and film critic. He was a member of the Cine-Club Vision where
he received his first film experience as an assistant director.

Upon the triumph of the Revolution, he worked as assistant
director on *This Our Land*. After writing and directing many

* The films described here, together with the two whose scripts are published in this volume, comprised the bulk of the aborted festival of
Cuban Films scheduled in March 1972.

documentaries, including *School in the Countryside* and *Story of a Battle*, he completed his first full-length feature, *La Salación*, in 1965. Since then he has directed the features *Tulipa, First Charge of the Machete* and, most recently, *Days of Water*.

In October, 1868, the Cubans rose against the occupying Spaniards in Oriente Province. The center of the uprising was the town of Bayamo. The Spaniards had guns and a trained army. The Cuban peasants had their machetes. This film is a kind of paean of praise to the machete as a weapon of liberation. Quite literally, this cane cutter was the only instrument the majority of the Cubans possessed with which they could fight. The story climaxes in a great battle of machete-wielding peasants against the occupying Spanish army. It is filmed entirely in contrasted black-and-white, to give the effect of viewing not a made-up filmed drama but a newsreel. It's as though you are seeing the events as they were photographed on the spot.

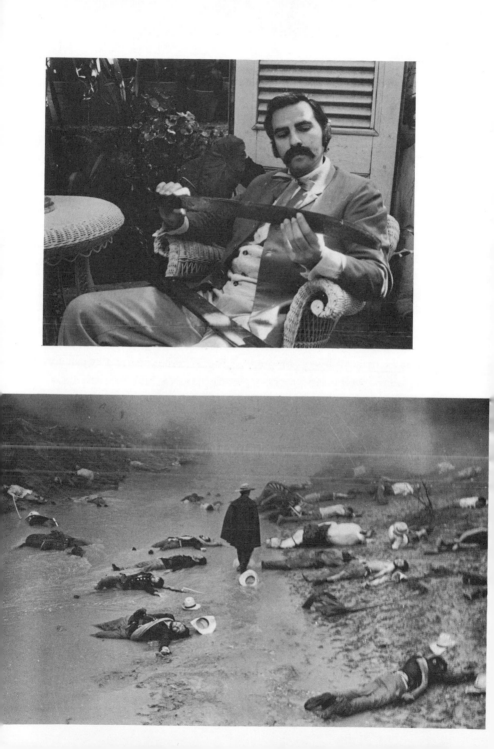

Director Manuel Octavio Gómez says, "I thought it would be interesting to deal with a historical event as if it were happening today, or better, as seen through the eyes of a person who would have been there as the events were taking place. It wasn't simply a formal intention, but a conceptual desire to make history more alive, more urgent. The style of the traditional historical film bothers me a great deal because I always find it rather museum-like, lifeless."

Le Monde said of *Primera Carga*, "Here is a film of great ingenuity, sculptured beauty, continually captivating. We will always remember the hymn of the machete, the Revolution's sacred weapon, and the final battle which broke the colonialists." And the London *Sunday Times* describes the film as "an exercise in historical reconstruction in more senses than one. The action is concerned with the fight against Spanish domination in the 1860s; by some special technical ingenuity the camera work has taken on . . . the shaggy-edged blacks and eye-straining whites of primitive photography; for a mad moment I began to wonder whether the motion picture camera had perhaps been already invented a century ago."

DAYS OF WATER *
Los Días del Agua

1971. Directed by Manuel Octavio Gómez; photographed by Jorge Herrera; edited by Nelson Rodríguez; screenplay by Manuel Octavio Gómez, Bernabe Hernández, Julio Garcia Espinosa; music by Leo Brower. With Idalia Anreus, Raúl

* This was the film confiscated by U.S. government agents to stop the Cuban Film Festival. Presumably it remains in a District of Columbia vault, perhaps next to some dark secrets of state.

Pomares, Adolfo Llauradó, Mario Balmaseda, and Omar Valdés. Color. Festivals: Gold Prize, Moscow 1971; London 1971.

Set in 1936, *Days of Water* tells the true story of a peasant woman who, after a visitation from the Virgin, claims the power of healing by the application of water which she blesses. Although a charlatan exploits her, she does appear to have healing powers which draw to her so many followers that she begins to have political influence. So much so that she is taken up by a local politician claiming to represent the common people. In fact, his ambitions are personal, and he liquidates the woman and her followers when these aims are achieved.

David Wilson, in the leading British film journal, *Sight and Sound*, writes: "Superman meets the Virgin Mary in *Days of Water*, and both are shot down by the guns of revolution. With them fall Disneyland and Coca-Cola, the political demagogue and the commercial charlatan, the decadence of the few and the disillusionment of the masses, all swept aside in a cathartic frenzy of destruction. In the orgiastic climax of this astonishing Cuban film, the blood of politics mingles with the red rose which a dying peasant saint clutches to her breast; religion and capitalism, twin bastions of centuries of exploitation, die together as the screen fills with red.

"*Days of Water* is a carnival, and as befits a carnival the finale stops the show. But long before the end, the eye has been dazzled by the spectacle, the sideshows as well as the big parade. Like the films of Glauber Rocha, this Cuban extravaganza shows the way to revolution in terms of mass culture. The violence of political upheaval on this scale is implicit in the heritage of black African ritual and Spanish Catholic ceremonial from which Cuban popular art takes its roots. And in the process the faded cardboard totems (and in the film they are just that) of an alien, North American culture are obliterated. What remains is all that is vital from a legacy almost destroyed by the corrosive influence of Church and State. It is an act of purification, an exorcism of black god and white devil performed not with water but with blood. . . .

"On a single viewing of this extraordinary film, one can do no more than point up its brilliant surface. Behind that surface lies an imagination which knows how to use cinema as a dynamic expression of popular art; and it has seldom been used to such astonishing effect."

THE ADVENTURES OF JUAN QUIN QUIN
Las Aventuras de Juan Quin Quin

1967. Written and directed by Julio Garcia Espinosa; photographed by Jorge Haydu; edited by Carlos Menéndez; music by Leo Brower, Luis Gómez, and Manuel Castillo. With Julio Martínez, Erdwin Fernández, and Adelaida Raymat. Cinemascope, black-and-white, 113 minutes. Festivals: Barcelona 1968; Pnom Penh 1969.

Julio Garcia Espinosa was born in 1926. He studied film direction at the Centro Sperimentale di Cinematografia in Rome. When the Revolution came to power, he was appointed Chief of the Art Section of the Rebel Army. He later became one of the founding members of ICAIC, for which he made several documentaries and feature-length films. In ICAIC's early years, his efforts were devoted to administrative matters, which kept him away from film-making for years. In 1967 he made *Adventures of Juan Quin Quin*. Two years later he traveled to the Democratic Republic of Vietnam to film *Third World, Third World War*.

Juan Quin Quin is a shrewd farmer in the days before the Revolution who fears nothing in his struggle to make his way. After a clash with his environment, the hero boldly faces innumerable situations which force him into varied occupations— an altar boy, a good man Friday in a circus, a bullfighter and, lastly, a professional revolutionary dedicated to the armed struggle against the government army.

Saturday Review, in an article about the suppressed New York festival, describes *Juan Quin Quin* as "An often-charming guerrilla-style spoof of spaghetti Westerns, which fluctuates between broad slapstick and serious revolutionary exposition. Actor Julio Martínez gives us an engaging Juan, the prerevolutionary flimflam man, a jack-of-all-trades who ekes out a meager living as altar boy, carny man, bullfighter, and tiller of the soil

until he is forced by boisterous, cartoonish imperialists into becoming a revolutionary Everyman. . . . At one point Juan gets caught in the machinery of the sugar mill; at another he escapes the clutches of the evil homosexual mill owner by jumping out a window and onto a waiting horse. . . . As *Juan* proceeds, we see that it is not to be just a Good-Guys-and-Bad-Guys burlesque. Godardesque titles and pop comic strips flash like fence posts to steer our minds toward business in the midst of pleasure. Then the serious stuff: Juan's sidekick Joseph and a pretty girl who shelters him from the enemy are killed. Finally, our hero responds. He is thoroughly radicalized."

Film maker Julio Garcia Espinosa has written, "I cannot conceive of language outside of its relation to an audience. . . . I wish to oppose the traditional structures of 'gaining consciousness.' That is, oppose those structures which don't afford people the opportunity to react, fight, confront; oppose them until they are no longer totally justified by the viewer. I think that we must abandon this type of dramatic structure once and for all. It is not necessary to *justify*, but to *stimulate* the people of our reality, our so-called Third World. Moreover, in this type of structure, the character never reacts until he reaches the point of total awareness. That is, until he bathes in those 'waters of the Jordan River' which signifies the 'grasping of consciousness.' On the contrary, I think that what must be attempted is to show that people are able to react without having reached a state of purity, of total awareness, without waiting for the famous 'grasping of consciousness.' "

THIRD WORLD
THIRD WORLD WAR
Tercer Mundo
Tercera Guerra Mundial

1970. Written and directed by Julio Garcia Espinosa; commentary by Roberto Fernández Retamar; photographed by Ivan Napoles and Luis Costelos; edited by Gloria Arguelles. Filmed in the Democratic Republic of Vietnam. Black-and-white, 90 minutes.

At the invitation of the War Crimes Commission of the Democratic Republic of Vietnam, a team of Cuban film makers

went to Vietnam from January 28 to March 11, 1970. Moving down to the 17th parallel, where they remained for a time, they literally faced the Americans. Their witness of this stay, in the form of reflection and disinterested analysis, is offered us by Espinosa. Roberto Fernández Retamar, the film's commentator, is one of Cuba's most important poets. A professor at Yale before the Revolution, he now is a director of Casa de las Americas, Cuba's prestigious publishing house devoted to Latin American literature. This intertwining of experiences—North American, Cuban, and Latin—underlies this essentially "Vietnamese" documentary.

Says *Le Monde*: "The frequent use of didactic titles *à la* Vertov and Solanas, the rejection of an underling's rhetoric, gives us in film an exemplary view. For the film makers, with the Vietnam war, symbol of Third World wars of liberation, the Third World War has begun."

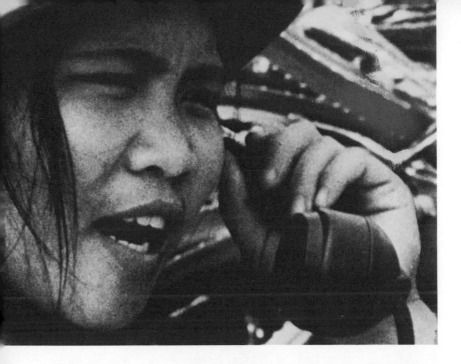

Espinosa, the director, explains his view of the relationship between his unabashedly partisan documentary and the Cuban audience: "Basically with this film we wanted to be rational and analytical. We did not exclude emotional qualities, but essentially it is directed to the reason of the audience. It is not an impressionistic film; it tries to spell out a process and its inner mechanisms. This process is the destructive war conducted by American imperialism against the Democratic Republic of Vietnam between 1965 and 1968. The idea was to give the most complete and coherent view of this war. Obviously South Vietnam is there too since, as we state in the film, it is the same war. At the same time the film shows the existence of a third world war in the Third World, taking Vietnam as the major example of this war. . . .

"*Third World, Third World War* is intended for an audience that has already taken a certain position. Therefore the film is not meant (although it does not exclude the possibility) to proselytize; it tries instead to heighten the consciousness and the experience of that revolutionary audience which in practice, in the actions of their everyday life, actually performs the function of convincing and proselytizing . . .

"Traditionally, leftist cinema presupposes an audience which is still unaware, and considers the film as a means to help it gain this awareness. To us, the public is the revolutionary who exists everywhere in the world, with a given level of awareness, since he is the man who is already fighting against American imperialism."

SHORTS AND DOCUMENTARIES

According to *The Guardian* (New York), "The great strength of Cuban documentary films is in their method of conveying political lessons (in the literal sense, carrying them to you) by all available means and yet without preaching. They raise consciousness with a poke, a jab, a seduction, a caress, a tack on the seat, the rapid-fire juxtaposition of all such techniques; not with a derrick. They raise the partitions between entertainment and instruction just as (and partly because) they reunite the eye and its intelligence. . . .

"Santiago Alvarez is the virtuoso of the Cuban documentarians . . . with his technique of jagged juxtaposition, quick but rarely obscure alternation of angles, Alvarez has brought the Brechtian method of epic didactic distance to its most brilliant film expression, with all the cogency and directness of which film as a medium is so uncommonly capable. And the epic documentary is a powerful form indeed: there is where art and propaganda melt together into communication, which is, after all, the function of communications media."

MANUELA

1966. Directed by Humberto Solás; photographed by Jorge Herrera; edited by Nelson Rodríguez; screenplay by Humberto Solás; music by Tony Tano. With Adela Legrá, Adolfo Llauradó, and Olga González. Black-and-white, 42 minutes. Festivals: Vina del Mar 1967; Cuneo (Italy) 1966.

Manuela is a peasant girl who joins the guerrillas in the Sierra Maestra after her mother has been murdered by Batista soldiers. Her sole desire is revenge. Humberto Solás, who later directed *Lucia*, shows in his first film the development of an uneducated natural person who is possessed by this one idea, and who changes into a disciplined revolutionary, capable even of showing pity for the soldiers who finally kill her. France's *Cinema 66* wrote of *Manuela*, "I could not contain the excitement upon discovering this masterpiece." (*photos p. 180 and opposite*)

TAKE-OFF AT 18:00
Despegue à las 18:00

1970. Directed by Santiago Alvarez. Black-and-white, 45 minutes.

This impressionistic study of the mass mobilization in Cuba to do battle in the war to eliminate underdevelopment is didactic but far from simple. The film's prologue shows one of Cuba's biggest problems, lines of people waiting for their rationed goods, only to find—*No Hay, No Hay*, "There Isn't Any, There Isn't Any." But then Alvarez also lets us know that *no hay* hunger, unemployment, polio, illiteracy. And with barely a catch of breath, the film takes off. The title refers to the 6 p.m. hour when voluntary labor begins and legions of *campesinos*, students, office and industrial workers put in extra hours to convert the island to a developed economy. Cuba derives its main ideological thrust from its own history of a century of intermittent armed struggle against first the Spanish, then a series of dictatorial regimes, culminating in the overthrow of Batista. Today—and in this film—the war against underdevelopment is seen as the latest and final battle of that continuum.

MADINA BOE

1969. Directed by José Massip. Black-and-white, 40 minutes.

A film essay on life in the liberated areas of Guinea-Bissau, the Portuguese colony in West Africa, and in the rearguard aid areas of the Republic of Guinea. Guerrilla camp life is fully documented, with guerrilla medicine, physical training, athletic matches, and political instruction. Included is footage of the results of NATO-supplied bomb attacks on the population and an interview with the late Amilcar Cabral, founder of the PAIGC independence movement.

FOR THE FIRST TIME
Por Primera Vez

ICAIC, 1967. Directed by Octavio Cortazar. Black-and-white, 12 minutes.

One of ICAIC's mobile projection crews goes by truck to a remote mountain village in Oriente Province to show the *campesinos* their first motion picture. (*photos opposite*)

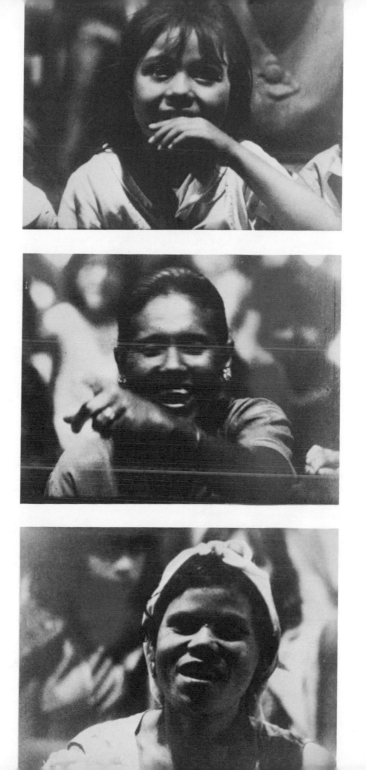

NOW!

ICAIC, 1965. Directed by Santiago Alvarez. Black-and-white, 5 minutes.

A short tribute to the U.S. civil rights struggle accompanied by the militant song "Now!" sung by Lena Horne. (*photo below*)

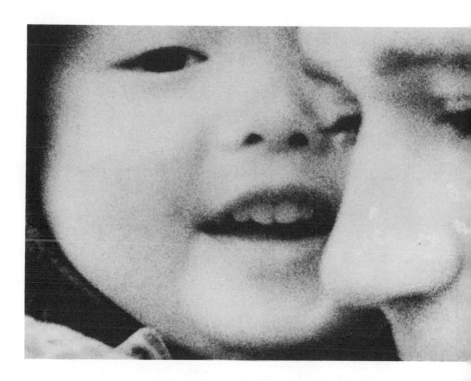

HANOI, TUESDAY THE 13TH
Hanoi, Martes Trece

ICAIC, 1967. Directed by Santiago Alvarez. Black-and-white, 40 minutes.

A visual record of Tuesday, December 13, 1966, in the lives of the Vietnamese in Hanoi and the rural outskirts of the city during the worst of U.S. bombing. (*photo above*)

79 SPRINGTIMES
79 Primaveras

ICAIC, 1969. Directed by Santiago Alvarez. Black-and-white, 25 minutes.

A brilliant impressionist biography of Ho Chi Minh, tracing his political career from 1920 to 1969, the last of his 79 springtimes. (*photo below*)

HISTORY OF A BALLET
Historia de un Ballet

ICAIC, 1969. Directed by Jorge Massip. Color, 20 minutes.

A photo-essay of the Cuban Ballet, which was formed under the direction of prima ballerina Alicia Alonzo. (*photo opposite*)

LAOS: THE FORGOTTEN WAR
La Guerra Olvidada

1967. Directed by Santiago Alvarez. Black-and-white, 20 minutes.

An incredible document of the spirit of the Lao people in the liberated areas of Laos. Under the continuing saturation bombing of the U.S., the people have transferred virtually all of their activities to cave living. They attend school, have a fully structured medical program, a cultural life of dancing and movies, and receive political and military training under the Pathet Lao leadership—all within a network of caves.

EVER ONWARD TO VICTORY
Hasta la Victoria Siempre

1965. Directed by Santiago Alvarez. Black-and-white, 28 minutes.

A televised speech by Che Guevara, intercut with photo and film montages. Che recalls the early days of the Cuban Revolution, and in a sequence given added meaning by his death, talks of the CIA and the U.S. Army role in Bolivia and Latin America. (*photo below*)

SCHOOL IN THE COUNTRYSIDE
La Escuela en al Campo

1961. Directed by Manuel Octavio Gómez. Black-and-white, 17 minutes.

A look at the new experimental schools designed to combine study and productive work. (*photo above*)

STORY OF A BATTLE
Historia de una Batalla

1961. Directed by Manuel Octavio Gómez. Black-and-white, 40 minutes.

A document of the Cuban campaign against illiteracy, launched in the first year of the revolutionary government, and carried out amid assassinations by counterrevolutionaries and the Bay of Pigs invasion. Waged by educated Cuban youth and progressive professionals, the campaign reached into urban slums and the most remote mountain areas of the island. (*photo below*)

DEATH TO THE INVADER
Muete al Invasor

1961. Directed by Santiago Alvarez. Black-and-white, 15 minutes.

The Bay of Pigs attack and the victory of the Cuban militia.

HOW AND WHY WAS
THE GENERAL MURDERED?
Como, Por Que y Para Que Se Asesina a un General?

1971. Directed by Santiago Alvarez. Black-and-white, 20 minutes.

An investigation of the murder of General Schneider, head of the Chilean armed forces, immediately following the electoral victory of Salvador Allende's socialist coalition government. The film documents the involvement of Chilean rightist circles, operating in concert with U.S. agencies. (*photo above*)

THE STAMPEDE
La Estampida

1971. Directed by Santiago Alvarez. Black-and-white, 12 minutes.

The U.S.-Saigon defeat in their 1971 invasion of Laos along

Route 9. In brilliant montage work, the Laotian victory is illustrated in newsreels, old film clips and animated cartoons, with music by Country Joe McDonald and The Fish.

CYCLONE

Ciclón

ICAIC, 1963. Directed by Santiago Alvarez. Black-and-white, 22 minutes.

A report, in pictures and music only, on the devastating effects of hurricane Flora in 1963, with Fidel Castro directing the relief operations. (*photo below*)

Posters

Documental cubano
Dirección: SANTIAGO ALVAREZ
Cámara: IVAN NAPOLES
Música: LEO BROWER

HANOI
MARTES 13

rostgaard/68

POSTERS

Anyone familiar with Western expositions on art in socialist countries knows it is always fashionable to stereotype "socialist realism," the critics out-vulgarizing the most vulgar of the genre under examination. This critical view has become the popular vision, imbuing millions in our country with a smug superiority toward socialist art—of which they have seen little if any—while Campbell Soup can faddists are promoted as new geniuses.

Many North Americans will argue the virtues of Czech films of the late 1960s as opposed to those of the Soviet Union. But for the most part the Czech films in favor are the three or four imported here at the selection of the U.S. State Department's cultural exchange people or commercial distributors; the judgment of Soviet films was based on imagination since none were selected for distribution here in that same period.

In just this way, some intellectuals of liberal bent, hoping against hope, moved to embrace the Cuban Revolution and its artists, as a revolutionary opposition to the Soviet Union. When Fidel Castro criticizes the cultural colonialism of "the literary parlors of New York and Paris" he is referring to this attempt by the fickle "friends" of Cuba to bring to the island their own prejudices; whose own cultural notions have been shaped by the bourgeoisies of their countries, rendering them incapable of judging the art and its function in a revolutionary situation, concretely and not metaphysically.

A veteran of the Abraham Lincoln Brigade, the U.S. volunteers who fought for the Republic in the Spanish Civil War, recalls a conversation with Herbert Matthews, *The New York Times* reporter who was himself a partisan of the Republican cause. Matthews had found a copy of Lenin's *State and Revolution*, had read through it and was puzzled. "What do you make of this?" asked the Princeton-educated journalist, adding, "I just don't get it." This book, which was standard fare for the Spanish workers fighting in the trenches at Madrid, was incomprehensible to *The New York Times* reporter. To Matthews' credit was his honesty, a quality he brought to all of his work. Most others passed judgment on phenomena—revolutions and their superstructures—they couldn't understand.

The poster, of course, is a slogan in images, making abstractions understandable. It meets these requirements: it is relatively inexpensive, and it can be viewed at one's own pace. In the United States today the poster has become another hip consumer item; bookstores and headshops in most cities do good business with a stock ranging from W. C. Fields to Agnew-with-long-hair, from Che Guevara to the latest Peter Max. This eclecticism might be seen as an ecumenical raising of consciousness. The contrary view, of course, is that it serves to blunt consciousness, to create a mindlessness wherein Che is reduced to just another charm on the consumer's bracelet. The poster fad came in with the 1960s rock culture, geared to the new lucrative youth market, both perhaps prototypical of McLuhan's anti-intellectual rejection of the printed word. If the printed word was passé, this was not because it was outdated by electronic media; rather, it could not be trusted. Statesmen, pontiffs, pedants all fashioned their latest lies with words, words, words. Some of the most imaginative, creative artists of our country were devoted to advertising the latest foreign car import or next year's candidate for U.S. senator. But, true to American profit-making, this very rejection of the distortions of mercantilism resulted in a new market.

Posters in Cuba are under the jurisdiction of the COR (the Party's Committee on Revolutionary Orientation) and the various institutes. The ones included here come, of course, from the ICAIC. Cuba is a country with a scarcity of consumer goods and an ideology which combats the consumer mentality. Commercials and advertisements are not to be found on the island; these film posters are announcements of new films produced or acquired. The Cuban audience will go, it needn't be sold. Public consciousness is expanded—not consumer appetites whetted—by the posters as by the films themselves.

The Cuban poster is itself not momentary—as is, say, the subway ad for the latest film at the Loews—but is an object unto itself. It is a supplement to the film, dessert as much as appetizer. Since Toulouse-Lautrec, at least, the poster has opened up a new art form. The October Revolution in Russia added revolutionary consciousness to the form for its takers. The form was then developed in most industrialized countries. But in Cuba, as with the film, there was no prerevolutionary tradition of poster art. Which makes the following all the more remarkable.

Director: Erich von Stroheim-USA 1924-cinemateca de cuba

AVARICIA

ñiko/71

EL
GABINETE
DEL DOCTOR
CALIGARI

Director: Robert Wiene
Alemania 1919
cinemateca de cuba

ñiko/71

AVENTURAS DE JUAN QUINQUIN

FILM CUBANO EN CINEMASCOPE   DIRECCION JULIO GARCIA ESPINOSA   CON JULIO MARTINEZ
ERDWIN FERNANDEZ/ADELAIDA RAYMAT/ENRIQUE SANTIESTEBAN

bachs/67

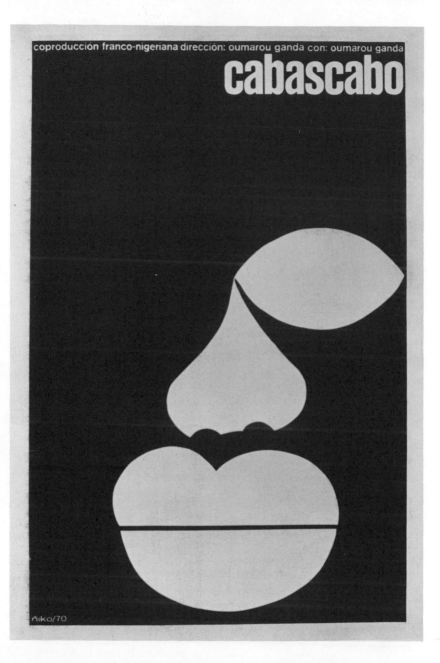

film anglonorteamericano dirección: john huston
con: montgomery clift susannah york larry parks

FREUD

azcuy 71

FILM SOVIETICO EN COLORES   Dirección: SERGUEI BONDARCHUK   Con: LUDMILA SAVELIEVA

LA GUERRA Y LA PAZ
(IV PARTE)

azcuy 69

The text of this book was set in Times Roman by Maryland Linotype Composition Co., Baltimore, Maryland. The display type is Optima. The book is printed on Sebago Antique by Murray Printing Co., Forge Village, Massachusetts, which also did the paperback binding. The clothbound edition was bound at The Colonial Press Inc., Clinton, Massachusetts. The typography was selected by Barbara Haner. Layout was designed by Aileen Friedman.